Dual Dichotomy 2023 ©

Scripture quotations are from:

Scripture quotations marked (AMPC) are taken from the Amplified Bible Classic, Old Testament, copyright © 1965, 1987 by the Zondervan Corporation. The Amplified Bible, New Testament, copyright © 1954, 1958, 1962, 1964, 1965, 1987 by the Lockman Foundation.

All Rights Reserved. No part of this publication may be reproduced or transmitted in any form or by any means, electronic or mechanical, including photocopy, recording, or any information storage and retrieval system, except for brief quotations in reviews, without the written permission of the author.

Cover & Paulette Denise Photo by Double Portion Photography

Printed in the United States of America

ISBN 978-0-9831341-6-8

Copyright © 2023 by Paulette Denise Turner

A Portion Ministries

Dual Introduction

The title: Dual Dicho**to***my* has dimensions of meaning. The word "dicho" in science means "in two parts or in two pairs." In English it means "saying or word". Hence, we are viewing two parts or pairs of sayings regarding identity AND renewal of the mind, contrasted "to" arrive at *"my"* authentic identity AND *"my"* authentic mental health status.

The cover is more than just a clipart picture. It is an actual photo that we took while on vacation in Alaska. I've always had an affinity for lighthouses, and found that they symbolize strength, safety, individuality, mystery, resilience, hope and security. All of these are qualities that enable human beings to overcome life's most formidable challenges and obstacles. As beacons of light, lighthouses provide guidance for safe passage to sailors and protect not only their lives but the land nearby. Additionally, lighthouses provide an earthly example of the spiritual principle of Jesus, the Light of the World, compared to a lighthouse. Lastly, the two main purposes of lighthouses are to serve as a navigational aid and to warn boats of dangerous areas. Join in on this journey of authentic identity and renewal of the mind, contrasted against mental health issues and addictions.

This is an academic Double Portion journey of the making of a dynamic Christian Counselor. This dual thesis project is a result of personal experience and extensive research to be made whole. The target audience for this thesis project would be to empower counselors, believers, and individuals on the dichotomies that hinder identity and renewal of the mind.

Unlike the other four volumes I've authored, this manuscript is written from an academic perspective. It is a combination of the two literal published theses submitted to Newburgh Theological Seminary.

The Dichotomy of Identity ⇆ Mental Health Issues

The Dichotomy of Renewal of the Mind ⇆ Addictions

I have combined the table of contents and bibliography; as well, the footnotes have been modified for printing ease (using the "ibid" function to denote the same previous reference point). Therefore, they are not in academic formatting, yet are still accurate references for crediting the source and for further study.

As stated above, the previous four books I've written were in volume style. Likewise, this thesis project has been grouped in volumes:

- **Volume One:** Single Women (Family Life Situations). In 2002.
- **Volume Two:** Christians On Assignment – Talking About Obedience. In 2010.
- **Volume Three:** Renewal Of The Mind According to Romans 12:2. In 2014.
- **Volume Four:** Kingdom Ready – Thy Kingdom Come. In 2018.
- **Thesis Volume One:** The Dichotomy Of Identity And Mental Health Issues. In 2021.
- **Thesis Volume Two:** The Dichotomy Of Renewal Of The Mind And Addictions. In 2023.
- **Volume Five:** The Truth About Holiness From The Heavenlies. TBD.

At the conclusion of the four volumes, my plans were to begin directly into the fifth volume, which I began with extensive studies and research. However, the Lord led me to complete my master's degree in Christian Counseling, followed by a dual doctorate program. Preparation time is never wasted time! What some may have viewed as delay was actually the Lord preparing me, healing me, and equipping me for the redefined task of volume five.

This twenty-one-year writing journey could be labeled: The Evolution of Authentic Belief. There are some things in the previous volumes that I now have a different viewpoint of, however, they have shaped me into where I am now (Compound Revelation and Abundant Grace). Some viewpoints go deeper and further than initially understood at the time of writing.

Conclusively, this journey has been orchestrated by Holy Spirit to constantly ignite curiosity and a hunger for truth, which leads to my next project: **Volume Five:** The Truth About Holiness From The Heavenlies. I've learned to not announce the projected date, as I did this at the conclusion of each previous four volumes, and NEVER completed as I thought, but within God's timeline for my life. Just know that Volume Five has dual PORTIONS:

1) The revelation *portion* based on scripture, and

2) The fictional story incorporating the principles exposed in the revelation *portion*.

About the author

Paulette Denise – no frills – just souled out love for Jesus Christ and His people. She is a prayer pioneer at heart, giving the word of God entrance into the lives of God's people through intercession. She also knows that preparation time is never wasted time.

Originally from Oakland, CA – yet has lived in Houston, TX since 2005. She has been in ministry since 1998. She married Don Turner in 2015. They have a blended family of 4 children and 6 grandchildren.

She graduated from Rhema Bible Training College; received her Bachelors degree in Business Management from University of Phoenix; her Masters & Doctorates of Philosophy in Christian Counseling from Newburgh Theological Seminary.

Dr. Paulette is the author of 4 books, co-author of 3, and helps other's birth their books. She flows in the gifts of the prophetic, administration, Christian Counseling, dance and worship, and is a phenomenal teacher of the Bible. She is the founder of **A Portion Ministries** in 1999, also, the co-founder of **Double Portion Kingdom Ministries** in 2015: a place of authentic salvation and deliverances.

DOUBLE PORTION KINGDOM MINISTRIES PURPOSE STATEMENT

A kingdom center for the people of God to gain a better understanding of the kingdom, the constitution of the kingdom (the word of God/Truth); and creating authentic disciples of Christ.

Table of Contents

Dual Introduction 1

About the author 6

Table of Contents 7

VOLUME ONE: THE DICHOTOMY OF IDENTITY AND MENTAL HEALTH ISSUES .. 12

Dedication and Acknowledgments 13

Abstract 14

Introduction 16

      Foundation of Righteousness 19

PART ONE: DICHOTOMY OF IDENTITY 22

CHAPTER ONE: The Community of God 22

    God is Love 26

    HuMANkind: Male and Female 28

CHAPTER TWO: Tri-part Being of HuMANkind 32

    Imago Dei 34

    Spirit 39

    Soul 42

    Body 46

CHAPTER THREE: Screwtape Element 50

PART TWO: DICHOTOMY OF MENTAL HEALTH 57

CHAPTER FOUR: Mental Health 57

    Statistics 57

    Identity Crisis 63

    Carnal Nature 65

    Distorted Identity – Through Fear, Rejection, ACEs, Trauma, and Rebellion 70

    The Brain 75

    Aftermath: Critical Spirit, Codependency, Anxiety – Depression, ADD, and Addictions 78

CHAPTER FIVE: Empowered Identity 85

    Salvation and Deliverance 85

    The Role of Holy Spirit 89

    Forgiveness 93

    Inner Healing 96

CHAPTER SIX: Summary and Conclusions 100

VOLUME TWO: THE DICHOTOMY OF RENEWAL OF THE MIND AND ADDICTIONS
.... 104

Dedication and Acknowledgments 105

Abstract 106

Introduction 108

    Defining Addictions 108

PART ONE: DICHOTOMY RENEWAL OF THE MIND 112

CHAPTER SEVEN: The Realm Of The Mind 112

    Renewal 112

    Mind/Soul 113

Early Formation 116

Conscience vs. Conscious 119

Guilt 125

Subconscious 129

The Thought Life And Strongholds 131

Feelings And Emotions 137

Biblical Survey Of Types Of Mind 144

CHAPTER EIGHT: Truth 147

The Spirit of Truth – Holy Spirit 147

Lies And Deception 151

CHAPTER NINE: Mind vs. Brain 153

Science of the Brain 153

Communication – Perception 155

CHAPTER TEN: Transformation 157

Guidelines for Transformation: 158

PART TWO: DICHOTOMY OF ADDICTIONS 159

CHAPTER ELEVEN: Possible Causes of Addictions 159

Demonic Influence 161

Passiveness or Aggressiveness 163

Unresolved Anger 165

Trauma – ACEs 168

Damaged Emotions 169

Memory Repression 171

Conflict Avoidance 173

Depression 173

Denial 176

CHAPTER TWELVE: Types of Addictions 178

CHAPTER THIRTEEN: The Brain And Addictions 186

The Brain 186

Epigenetics 188

Dopamine 190

CHAPTER FOURTEEN: Bodywork 193

Healing Systems 193

Another Look At Dopamine 195

CHAPTER FIFTEEN: Tool For Renewal Of The Mind 197

Healed Emotions 198

Renewed Thoughts 201

Breaking Cycles 203

True Identity 206

Healthy Coping Mechanisms 209

Bibliotherapy 211

Love 213

Joy 215

Humility 216

Forgiveness 217

Authenticity 220

Prayer 221

Obedience And Meekness 222

CHAPTER SIXTEEN: Summary and Conclusions..224
APPENDIX A: Worksheet for Renewal Of The Mind 227
Combined Bibliography 231

VOLUME ONE: THE DICHOTOMY OF IDENTITY AND MENTAL HEALTH ISSUES

Paulette Denise Turner

Newburgh Theological Seminary

Doctor of Philosophy in Christian Counseling

September 2, 2021

Dichotomy ONE: Dedication and Acknowledgments

"For Ezra had prepared and set his heart to seek the Law of the Lord [to inquire for it and of it, to require and yearn for it], and to do and teach in Israel its statutes and its ordinances." (Ezra 7:10 Amplified Classic, AMPC)

Above all I want to acknowledge the Divine Community of God: Father, Son, and Holy Spirit. In loving dedication to the memory of Larry Michael Blue Sr. for prompting me to explore and share the "choo-choo" train revelations that have become a spiritual trademark in my life, and evident in this project. Additionally, this manuscript is dedicated to my husband and immediate family: Thank you for unconditional support throughout this extensive process.

A special thanks to those who were a sounding board for the concepts developed here. To Donald Turner and Twinkle Francis for your dedication in proof reading ALL of the papers in the Master's and Doctor of Philosophy program here at Newburgh Theological Seminary these past three years.

Dichotomy ONE: Abstract

Background

Many believers are suffering with mental health issues; for apparently unknown reasons. A root cause for some of these mental health issues is the lack of authentic identity (Imago Dei).

Aim

The purpose of this study was to contrast the dichotomy of identity with the presenting mental health issues. The resulting goal is to empower Christian Counselors with this wisdom and knowledge to be able to assist people to understand authentic identity, or Imago Dei.

Methods

A collective method of contrasting exploratory and analytical research of various respected researchers was used. Along with an experimental conference session in which participants were exposed to the hypothesis and shared input on the topic.

Results

This study proved that identity and mental health issues are directly correlated. The identification or lack there of regarding identity as the Imago Dei can be helpful in empowering believers to walk in their empowered identity.

Conclusions

Empowering Christian Counselors with this tool to identify identity breaches in their counselees will help reduce mental health issues.

Dichotomy ONE: Introduction

"God-lovers make the best counselors. Their words possess wisdom and are right and trustworthy. The ways of God are in their hearts and they won't swerve from the paths of steadfast righteousness (Psalm 37:30-31 TPT)."

Merriam Webster dictionary defines **dichotomy** as: "a division into two especially mutually exclusive or contradictory groups or entities. Something with seemingly contradictory qualities."[1] This project will review the contradictory qualities of identity and mental health issues. Additionally, we will introduce the notion that an effective Christian counselor will be aware of the fundamentals of identity and have the capacity to identify identity blockages. Therefore, being able to effectively address, minister, and counsel through mental health issues that are present; and provide healing, deliverance, and spiritual direction.

"In our everyday world, a problem is something we try to avoid. But in academic research, a problem is something we seek out, even invent. Indeed, without a problem to work on, a researcher is out of work."[2] The problems this research project will be addressing are the various mental health issues that can be resolved by balancing the dichotomy of identity.

To the degree that a person is unclear, unaware, or lacking an understanding of their identity, mental health issues may manifest. A competent Christian counselor will be able to

---

[1]. Merriam Webster Dictionary

[2]. Kate L. Turabian, *A Manual for Writers of Research Papers, Theses, and Dissertations: Chicago Style for Students and Researchers*, 9th ed. (Chicago: University of Chicago Press, 2018), 17.

assess the breach in identity, determine the root, and be able to deal with the mental health issue; the fruit.

Hosea says: "Hear the word of the Lord, you children of Israel, for the Lord has a controversy (a pleading contention) with the inhabitants of the land, because there is no faithfulness, love, pity and mercy, or knowledge of God [from personal experience with Him] in the land. There is nothing but [false] swearing and breaking faith and killing and stealing and committing adultery; they break out [into violence], one [deed of] bloodshed following close on another … **My people are destroyed for lack of knowledge**; because you [the priestly nation] have rejected knowledge, I will also reject you that you shall be no priest to Me; seeing you have forgotten the law of your God, I will also forget your children. The more they increased and multiplied [in prosperity and power], the more they sinned against Me; I will change their glory into shame. They feed on the sin of My people and set their heart on their iniquity (Hosea 4:1-2, 6-8 AMPC, emphasis added)."

I toiled to hone in the first dichotomy as identity, because it is easier summarized as the Imago Dei. Catherine Skurja (of The Imago Dei Ministries), in her book *Paradox Lost* helped bring clarity to this toil: "As ambassadors entrusted with his message of reconciliation (2 Corinthians 5:14-21), we are to represent God to the world. But when we define ourselves outside of Him, that message gets muddled. Not only do we live without the freedom Christ died to give us, we are not able to help others find their true identity, either. What would life be like if you were who you were? What if the one thing you knew unshakably, deep in your heart, was that you are the Beloved of God?"[3]

Identity (Imago Dei) is a foundation of salvation. For a person to know that they are created in the image of God, and He has redeemed us to operate as such is profound. Therefore, believers will be tested to see if they have truly learned the lesson of identity. James Lee Beall, in his book titled: *Laying The Foundation Achieving Christian Maturity* describes the role of tests in the following manner: "Tests are a part of education too. They are not meant to be an occasion for tension. They will help you find out whether you are learning. They will point out your strengths and weaknesses in order to help you do something about them…Let tests teach you."[4] Also, know that God doesn't test people with sin, but He tests them to walk out the word that they have been taught and exposed to.

Comparative to the banking industry, their employees' study authentic money to enable them to recognize any counterfeit money. They do not study counterfeit first, only after a foundation of the authentic is laid. In like manner, counselors should understand true identity centered in the Imago Dei and be able to recognize the counterfeits of mental health issues that arise. This recognition of identity will permit the counselor to address the root issues instead of (or in correlation to) the manifesting fruit.

---

[3] Catherine Skurja. *Paradox Lost: Uncovering the True Identity in Christ*. (Imago Dei Resources LLC, 2012). 35.

[4] James L. Beall, and Marjorie Barber. *Laying the Foundation*. (Bridge Logos Fndtn, 1976). Xxvi.

Foundation of Righteousness

I learned a principle at Rhema Bible Training College in March 2002 that has stuck with me and morphed into how I view identity. Initially, I was unaware of the weight of this concept about the foundation of righteousness. This principle must be taught from the bottom up, not the reverse, building upon the foundation of the Trinity of God.

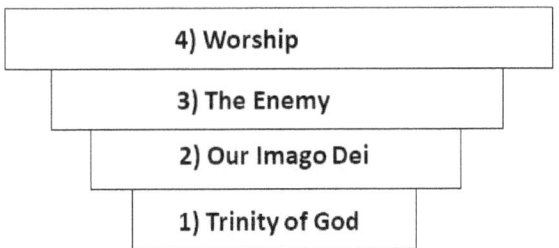

1) Trinity of God. At Rhema, the only focus was on knowing the Father. However, I have expanded it to knowing the entire Trinity of God. God the Father – God the Son – God the Holy Spirit. The Community of God. A foundational understanding of the Trinity of God must be laid for a person to truly grasp identity. **2) Our Imago Dei.** The fact that human beings are created in the image of God as image bearers. According to Richard Rohr, the capacity to mirror the Divine Three is lost "in our on-the-ground understanding of who God is and who we therefore are, created in God's image and likeness"[5]. Rightly so, these first two elements of understanding identity and that believers have the capacity to "become the righteousness of God through our union with Him (2 Corinthians 5:21b, AMPC)" must be taught to believers first, before the next component.

---

[5] Richard Rohr and Mike Morrell. *The Divine Dance: The Trinity and Your Transformation*. (Whitaker House, 2016. Kindle edition). 28.

3) The enemy. For now just know that there is an adversary, and he is NOT equal to the Trinity of God. **4) Worship.** The ancient battle is about worship. The conflict in Genesis 3, and in the tempting of Jesus in Luke 4 exposes the battle that is rooted in identity. These first three elements will be explained in-depth in the next chapter.

In his chapter on *God's Army of Worshippers*, Francis Frangipane says "indeed, no one can do warfare who is not first a worshiper of God."[6] It is said that worship protects the heart of believers. "A plain definition of 'worship' is man's response to the revelation of who God is — as we grow in knowing who God is and who we are in Him, our worship experience should deepen and heighten. This is when it no longer requires a church building or a cheerleader to tell us to worship God, because we are growing and knowing who God is."[7]

This previous quote was written in 2013. However, in the aftermath of the COVID-19 pandemic and global shut in, this is more evident. "In these closing moments of this age, the Lord will have a people whose purpose for living is to please God with their lives. In them, God finds His own reward for creating man. They are His worshipers. They are on earth only to please God, and when He is pleased, they also are pleased. The Lord takes them farther and through more pain and conflicts than other men… When they are crushed, like the petals of a flower, they exude a worship, the fragrance of which is so beautiful and rare that angels weep in quiet awe at their surrender. They are the Lord's purpose for creation."[8]

---

[6] Francis Frangipane. *The Three Battlegrounds: An In-Depth View of the Three Arenas of Spiritual Warfare: the Mind, the Church and the Heavenly Places*, 2nd ed. (Cedar Rapids: Arrow Publications, 2010). 89.

[7] Paulette Denise. *Renewal of the Mind! According to Romans 12:2*. (A Portion Ministries, 2014). 213.

[8] Francis Frangipane. *The Three Battlegrounds: An In-Depth View of the Three Arenas of Spiritual Warfare: the Mind, the Church and the Heavenly Places*, 2nd ed. (Cedar Rapids: Arrow Publications, 2010). 93.

These four foundations of righteousness are a profound anchor for the premise of this project. Therefore, the dichotomy of this research project is to discuss the multi-dimensions of identity in PART ONE; and the multi-dimensions of mental health issues in PART TWO.

PART ONE: DICHOTOMY OF IDENTITY
CHAPTER ONE: The Community of God

I like the way John MacArthur addresses the Trinity of God in his book *Worship, the Ultimate Priority:* "God is one, yet He is three. I haven't got the faintest idea how to explain that divine mystery to everyone's complete satisfaction, but my own inability to articulate it in a way that answers everyone's questions doesn't diminish my faith in God or my conviction that He exists as One in three Persons."[9] Richard Rohr contrasts the need for having an understanding of the relationship of the Persons of the godhead by stating, "Bad theology is like pornography – the imagination of a real relationship without the risk of one ... It dehumanizes God and turns the wonder and the messy mystery of intimate relationship into a centerfold to be used and discarded."[10] Believers must have a healthy foundation of the Trinity of God, the Community of God.

The goal with this section of the research is to provide a panorama of the many aspects of the relational God Who is a being, Who is transcendent and immanent as a spirit, and as a person. Three in one = Trinity. Or as the book the *Divine Dance* states it, "If we take the depiction of God in *The Trinity* seriously, we have to say, 'In the beginning was the Relationship.'"[11] Catherine Skurja speaks of this relationship of three being one in essence, but

---

[9] John F. MacArthur *Worship: The Ultimate Priority*. (Chicago: Moody Publishers, 2012). 77.

[10] Richard Rohr and Mike Morrell. *The Divine Dance: The Trinity and Your Transformation*. (Whitaker House, 2016. Kindle edition). 19.

[11] Richard Rohr and Mike Morrell. *The Divine Dance: The Trinity and Your Transformation*. (Whitaker House, 2016. Kindle edition). 27.

distinct in personality. However, "a broken and divided understanding of God leads to a broken understanding of self and broken relationship with other people."[12]

To expound on the relevance of the broken view of God, I conducted an informal survey during a conference event. The focus of the conference was regarding this element of thesis topic to determine how attendees viewed and rated the attributes of each member of the Trinity. After sharing several wisdom keys regarding the Persons of the Trinity, the survey material was given using the criteria discussed by Catherine Skurja in her chapter on The Triune Life.[13] The following are the results from the attendees:

	Approachable	Stern/Just	Friendly	Comforting	Powerful	Creative
God The Father	1	9	1	2	8	4
God The Son	9	2	9	4	2	1
God The Holy Spirit	3	2	2	7	3	7

[14]

My findings varied from Catherine Skurja in that most of the students she surveyed viewed God the Father as stern/just and powerful, and least approachable and comforting. While those I surveyed viewed God the Father as most approachable. Our findings match on God the Son being most friendly and approachable. Regarding God the Holy Spirit, those I surveyed identified with Him as comforting and creative, as well as friendly and approachable.[15]

---

[12]Catherine Skurja. *Paradox Lost: Uncovering the True Identity in Christ*. (Imago Dei Resources LLC, 2012). 58.
[13] Ibid. 59.
[14] Paulette D. Turner, *Identity Conference via Zoom*. (Conference session April 10, 2021).
[15] Ibid.

Richard Rohr and Mike Morrell narrated stupendously in their description of the Russian iconographer Andrei Rublev's fifteenth century icon titled *The Trinity*, inserted below in black and white. "In Rublev's icon there are three primary colors, which illustrate faces of the Holy One, all contained in Three."[16] I derived this chart for a quick glance of a few of the meanings emphasized by Rohr, and from personal knowledge:

FATHER	**SON**	**SPIRIT**
Gold	*Blue*	*Green*
Kingship. Perfection, fullness, wholeness, the ultimate Source.	Divinity. The Human. Sea and sky mirroring one another. God in Christ taking on humanity. A joining of divinity and humanity.	Quality of divine aliveness that makes everything blossom and bloom. The divine photosythesis that grows everything from within by transforming light into itself. The color of Pentecost.

The icon depicts a meal, which is a relational event. The open seat at the table is like "an invitation to share at the divine table; probably the first biblical hint of what we would eventually call *salvation*."[17]

Stanley Grenz shares comprehensively in his book *Theology for the Community of God* which is a foundation for understanding how "the three members of the Trinity build an eternal, ontological unity in diversity. Thereby Father, Son, and Spirit together comprise the divine being and essence. Theologians sometimes employ the term *perichoresis* to refer to the

---

16 Richard Rohr and Mike Morrell. *The Divine Dance: The Trinity and Your Transformation*. (Whitaker House, 2016. Kindle edition). 26.
17 Ibid 28.

interrelation, partnership, and mutual dependence of the Trinitarian members not only in the workings of God in the world but even more foundationally in their very subsistence as the one God."[18]

Ontologically, "The Father functions as the ground of the creation of the world, the Son is the Word, the principle of creation, through whom the Father creates. And the Spirit is the divine power active in bringing the world into existence."[19] Michael Heiser puts it this way in his book *The Unseen Realm, Recovering the Supernatural Worldview of the Bible:* "God's divine council is an assembly *in the heavens*, not on earth."[20]

Correlating to the discussion on the foundations of righteousness, Grenz offers: "The likeness of God, in contrast, is a supernatural gift. It is the original righteousness God bestowed on Adam in the Garden, which enabled the first human to use his reason to control his *lower powers* – the emotions and the appetites. In the fall, Adam lost this likeness to God, this supernatural gift."[21] Through the loss of identity, the supernatural gift was traded for a counterfeit gift; and through the regaining of foundational identity, access to these unseen realms can be possible again.

---

[18] Stanley J. Grenz *Theology for the Community of God.* (Grand Rapids: Wm. B. Eerdmans Publishing, 2000). 170

[19] Michael S. Heiser *The Unseen Realm: Recovering the Supernatural Worldview of the Bible.* (Lexham Press, 2015). 67.

[20] Michael S. Heiser *The Unseen Realm: Recovering the Supernatural Worldview of the Bible.* (Lexham Press, 2015). 29.
[21] Ibid. 170.

God is Love

All of this is inspired from the motive of love for mankind. "The divine image is essentially a special relation with the Creator which Adam lost, but Christ restores."[22] The crux of understanding the moral attributes of love is the manifesto of *God is love*. I have also discovered several theological inferences to love and the Trinitarian doctrine as: love as the essence of God; love and the divine holiness, jealousy and wrath; love and other moral attributes. These inferences also encompass "terms such as *grace, mercy, and long-suffering* – terms which speak of God's goodness…Above all, because God loves, He seeks the salvation and renewal of fallen creation."[23]

Human identity originated in God as depicted in the following scripture: "So that they should seek God, in the hope that they might feel after Him and find Him, although He is not far from each one of us. **For in Him** we live and move and have our being; as even some of your [own] poets have said, For we are also His offspring (Acts 17:28 AMPC, emphasis added)."

This concept is clearly spelled out in the beginning of the story of the descendants of Adam: "This is the book of the generations of Adam. **On the day when God created man, He made him in the likeness of God. He created them male and female**, and He blessed them and named them "mankind" on the day when they were created (Genesis 5:1-2 NASB, emphasis added)."

---

[22] Michael S. Heiser *The Unseen Realm: Recovering the Supernatural Worldview of the Bible*. (Lexham Press, 2015). 171.
[23] Ibid. 74.

It is in the Trinity of God, the community of God that we live and move. "We derive personal meaning from a reality beyond ourselves, for God bestows meaning on us. And this bestowed meaning is related to the goal, purpose, or destiny God intends for us. This is the deeper meaning of Paul's statement that in God we *have our being*."[24]

In Him we dance a Divine Dance. "Whatever is going on in God is a *flow*, a *radical relatedness*, a *perfect communion* between Three – a circle dance of love. And God is not just a dancer; God is the dance itself."[25] This describes the Divine Dance of love, or the *"divine circle dance*, as the early Fathers of the church dared to call it [in Greek *perichoresis*, the origin of our word *choreography*] ... May our ears be opened to the music that heals, celebrating the entanglement of differences so that even in our discord, we hear that we ourselves are the melody embraced in Three-Part Harmony."[26]

Another essential point to consider is the disintegration of the understanding of the Community of God. "The sinful destruction of community has been the human predicament from the beginning. The transgression of our first parents led to the unmistakable disruption of community. Their act brought alienation or estrangement where once had been only fellowship. The innocent transparency in the presence of each other they had once known gave way to shame *Genesis 3:7*. In addition, Adam and Eve now feared the face of the God

---

[24] Michael S. Heiser *The Unseen Realm: Recovering the Supernatural Worldview of the Bible*. (Lexham Press, 2015). 140.
[25] Richard Rohr and Mike Morrell. *The Divine Dance: The Trinity and Your Transformation*. (Whitaker House, 2016. Kindle edition). 24.
[26] Richard Rohr and Mike Morrell. *The Divine Dance: The Trinity and Your Transformation*. (Whitaker House, 2016. Kindle edition), 21, 27.

who had lovingly created them *Genesis 3:10*. And they experienced the bitter reality that the world around them was no longer their friend *Genesis 3:15, 17-19*."[27]

HuMANkind: Male and Female

Equally as important to understanding the unity of the community of God, is understanding that the Divine Community created huMANkind in His image; as well as male and female. Male and female is the gender, not a class delineation. Both the male and female huMAN were given the mandate to subdue and take dominion. "And God said, 'Let Us make huMANkind in Our image and according to Our likeness, and let them rule over the fish of the sea, and over the birds of heaven, and over the cattle, and over all the earth, and over every moving thing that moves upon the earth.' So God created huMANkind in His image, in the likeness of God He created him, male and female He created them. And God blessed THEM, and God said to THEM, "Be fruitful and multiply, and fill the earth and subdue it, and rule over the fish of the sea and the birds of heaven, and over every animal that moves upon the earth (Genesis 1:26-28 LEB, emphasis added)." This concept was also seen earlier when we looked at Genesis 5:1-2.

In creating huMANkind male and female, the principle that "femininity and masculinity consists of unique and deeply embedded ways of relating"[28] is evident. The

---

[27] Stanley J. Grenz *Theology for the Community of God*. (Grand Rapids: Wm. B. Eerdmans Publishing, 2000). 188.

[28] Larry Crabb. *Fully Alive: A Biblical Vision of Gender That Frees Men and Women to Live Beyond Stereotypes*. (Grand Rapids: Baker Books, 2013. Kindle edition). 33.

statement that Larry Crabb made of: "the relational Being creates relational human beings,"[29] gives deeper meaning to the fact that 'be fruitful and multiply' is a relational command which involves more than one human being. Part of laying the foundation of identity is to recognize the distinguished differences between males and females.

Gaining a knowledge that "an authentically masculine man is a man so grateful for his call to move toward others with the weight of divine impact that he confronts his paralyzing fear of weightlessness by relating in order to: hear the struggles of another; remember his privileged opportunity to move toward another and to do for another whatever he discerns will reveal the nature of God who sees the worst in another, feels its impact on Him, and yet refuses to back away; explore the depths of that struggle until he is aware of no stronger ambition than to be with another in unthreatening presence; sacrifice himself for the pleasure of serving the needs of another. He relates with one embraced purpose in mind: to encourage others to trust and to rest in the beauty of the God who is always moving toward others in love."[30]

In like manner, "an authentically feminine woman is a woman so at rest in God's delight in her indestructible beauty that she refuses to be a slave to her fear of invisibility. She therefore invites others to enjoy the beauty of God whose love casts out the power of fear as she relates: invitationally, not controllingly; openly, not guardedly; courageously, not defensively; freely, not protectively. She relates with one embrace purpose in mind: to encourage others to be consumed and transformed by the beauty of the God who sees, invites, nourishes, and enjoys His people."[31] The goal is to have both the male and female interact in

---

[29] Larry Crabb. *Fully Alive: A Biblical Vision of Gender That Frees Men and Women to Live Beyond Stereotypes*. (Grand Rapids: Baker Books, 2013. Kindle edition). 34.
[30] Ibid. 219.
[31] Ibid. 217-218.

such a way to apprehend that God "wants us to meet on the bridge built by His cross, the bridge on which men and women can connect by relating to each other in a way that reveals how God relates."[32]

Another author described these roles of femininity and masculinity as follows: "The development of both the feminine and masculine potentials in a person is also important for wholeness. The masculine aspect of personality may be variously described as logos, our outgoing reason, active creativity, controlled aggressiveness, psychological firmness, the capacity to strive for goals and overcome obstacles en route. The feminine aspect of personality comprises eros, or the capacity for relationships, understanding, awareness of others, creativity through receptiveness, an indirect way of attaining goals, patience, compassion, the valuing and nourishing of life. Everyone, man or woman, contains possibilities for both masculine and feminine development, and no one can approach wholeness without some development in both areas."[33]

As a dynamic kingdom minister, I was intrigued to find "the primary division in a human being is the masculine-feminine division, a primary symbol of the kingdom is that of the wedding, as we have seen. In a wedding male and female unite in one. From an external point of view this is only a sexual union, made possible by physical intercourse. From the psychological point of view the sexual act itself is an image of a higher unity that can take place within the individual as the diverse parts become one with each other…The mystery to which Paul refers to in Ephesians 5:31-32 is the mystery of the undivided, or androgynous

---

[32] Ibid. 42.

[33] John L. Sandford, and Paula Sandford. *Healing the Wounded Spirit*. (Victory House Publishers, 1985). 21.

person, one in whom division has been replaced by unity. No human being is pure masculinity or femininity, but each person contains elements of both…The union of masculine and feminine is therefore the symbol for the union of the psyche, and the image of the marriage is, naturally, the primary representation of their inner mystery."[34]

In his discussion on 1 Peter 3:1-2, Larry Crabb says "a woman has been opened by God to receive *whatever advances His purposes.* Jesus was opened, as the Son who loved His Father, to do His Father's will. For Him, that meant Calvary. A godly wife is called to likewise submit like Jesus – whose primary purpose was to reveal His Father's heart and holiness. I hear Peter telling women, *discern what you can do and say that most clearly reveals something beautiful about God that your husband needs to see, with the prayer that God will use your submission to further His will in your husband's life.* Don't be guided by what you most want your husband to do, or by what you most fear he might do, but rather by your openness to God to reveal what most represents the holy God of love."[35] Shame and fear distort and destroy masculinity and femininity and block the capacity to receive and operate in love.

Another aspect to be aware of in the male and female huMANkind is that of selfishness. "Before God's Spirit pours Christ's life into us, selfishness is the primary energy in the human soul"[36] due to the fall in Genesis 3. Larry Crabb states "self-centered relating – relational sin – destroys community."[37] This is why an understanding of the Community of God is needed, and we will now look at the community of the tri-part being of huMANkind.

---

[34] John L. Sandford, and Paula Sandford. *Healing the Wounded Spirit.* (Victory House Publishers, 1985). 165-165.
[35] Ibid. 60.
[36] Ibid. 30.
[37] Ibid. 129.

CHAPTER TWO: Tri-part Being of HuMANkind

HuMANkind was created in the image of God in Genesis 1:26-28, and God is a spirit. In the second chapter of Genesis God created the body for man at verse 7; then for woman at verses 21-22. The creation story was concluded as "And the man and his wife were both naked and were not embarrassed or ashamed in each other's presence (Genesis 2:25 AMPC)." The love light of God was the spiritual covering which suppressed the nakedness of man. This not only referred to a natural nakedness, but a spiritual nakedness and absence of light, or lack of identity (see Genesis 3:7 and 2:25). Since God clothed Himself with light as with a garment, as in Psalm 104:2, we can deduce that the man and woman were clothed in God's love. Deception and sin caused darkness in huMANkind's understanding of the love of God. The result was the distorted view or concept of the Community of God.

"And may the God of peace Himself sanctify you through and through [separate you from profane things, make you pure and wholly consecrated to God]; and may your **spirit** and **soul** and **body** be preserved sound and complete [and found] blameless at the coming of our Lord Jesus Christ (the Messiah) (1 Thessalonians 5:23 AMPC, emphasis added)."

The spirit can be viewed as <u>what you are</u>; the soul can be viewed as <u>who you are</u>; and the body can be viewed as <u>what you have</u>. The aspect of **WHAT** YOU ARE is the fact that you are created in the image of God. However, within the soul, the aspect of **WHO** YOU ARE is an element of the heart which is sometimes referred to as the spirit. When we speak of identity, we are addressing the identity as a tri-part being. The spirit of man was created in the image of God. The soul must be renewed; which is a constant happening from the time of awareness until a person is absent from the body and present with Christ.

"I appeal to you therefore, brethren, and beg of you in view of [all] the mercies of God, to make a decisive dedication of your bodies [presenting all your members and faculties] as a living sacrifice, holy (devoted, consecrated) and well pleasing to God, which is your reasonable (rational, intelligent) service and spiritual worship. Do not be conformed to this world (this age), [fashioned after and adapted to its external, superficial customs], but be transformed (changed) by the [entire] renewal of your mind [by its new ideals and its new attitude], so that you may prove [for yourselves] what is the good and acceptable and perfect will of God, even the thing which is good and acceptable and perfect [in His sight for you] (Romans 12:1-2 AMPC)."

This text is referring to the fact that the spirit is born again, and you must renew your mind (the heart here in this text) to be able to receive from the spirit. The heart appears in both the spirit and the soul realm. Know that the mind being renewed builds a strong heart. Consider the fact that Romans 10:9-10 says 'if you believe in your heart,' this is referring to the soulish realm, where the believing takes place — and what are beliefs? Beliefs are thoughts; a person uses their intellect and their reasoning to have faith in God. Therefore, the mind must constantly be renewed so that a person's faith in God can grow. That is how the little mustard seed grows and matures into a large oak tree.

The Holy Spirit, who is the Spirit of Truth will help us renew our mind. The Holy Spirit will teach and show you the matters of the heart, whether in the spirit or soul realm. Yet the Screwtape Element does not want us to renew our mind because the enemy knows that as long as he can keep us stuck on wrong beliefs with stinking thinking, with dead decaying thoughts, he can play games with us. But not so! The Lord is exposing it!

The soul causes us to be unique. The mind must be renewed according to the word of God, not religion; through sanctification which is the process of transformation. It was the soulish realm that lived on apart from God, and that is how the thoughts got distorted. The bible exposes that our thoughts and ways are not the same as God's: "For *My* thoughts about mercy are not like your thoughts, and *My* ways are different from yours (Isaiah 55:8 TPT, capitalization and emphasis added)." This is important because "when people see themselves the way God sees them, as His wonderful works and particular reflections of His image, then they see what is inside of them and perceive the universe in a different way, see Psalm 139:14."[38]

Imago Dei

In light of all that has been discussed thus far in PART ONE of this paper: the Community of God, the fact that huMANkind were created male and female as tri-part beings, we can now gain an understanding of the significance of knowing the Imago Dei. Furthermore, Imago Dei can be referred to as mankind's spiritual identity, made in the image of God, as image bearers. "The Imago Dei is also the *location* of our spiritual center. It is the 'place' within us where we connect with the Spirit of God or 'indwelling' God."[39]

Imago Dei embellishes the root understanding of male and female, He created them; He created huMANkind. "The fifth century theologian Augustine of Hippo wrestled with this idea. Based on his study of Genesis 1:26-27 and other scriptures, Augustine coined the Latin

---

[38] Caroline Leaf. *The Perfect You: A Blueprint for Identity*. (Ada: Baker Books, 2017). 33.
[39] Catherine Skurja. *Paradox Lost: Uncovering the True Identity in Christ*. (Imago Dei Resources LLC, 2012). 49.

phrase *Imago Dei*, meaning '*image of God.*' He stated that we are created 'to be the image of the Trinity; not equal to the Trinity as the Son is equal to the Father.' There is no such thing as a human being who is not created in the image of God. Therefore, the *Imago Dei* is the intrinsic and incorruptible value of each person."[40] All of huMANkind are created with Imago Dei, in the next section we will discuss hindrances to recognizing this truth; the Screwtape Element.

"The story of the Bible is about Gods will for, and rule of, the realms He has created, visible and invisible, through the imagers He has created, human and nonhuman."[41] Let Us make huMANkind in Our image and according to Our likeness. "The goal was to care for the earth and harness its gifts for the betterment of fellow human imagers, all the while enjoying the presence of God."[42]

A unique way that Catherine Skurja uses to describe the "prism" element of Imago Dei within each person is through the Paradox Lost demonstration of M&M© candies. The center (the Imago Dei) is the peanut, which is covered by the chocolate (the shameful and hurtful things that occur in life, especially in childhood, often referred to as 'crap' or dung), and the hard candy coating (depicting the masks we wear to cover the 'crap' and shame from others) to complete the M&M©. She also compares Imago Dei to the prism of a diamond. "The image of God in each person is always there, and its value never changes. Unfortunately, we spend a lot of time stuck in the dung, unaware of the true value of the diamond. We are all stuck in the dung, we do not see ourselves as God sees us. Jesus goes to great lengths in word

---

[40] Ibid. 35-36.
[41] Michael S. Heiser *The Unseen Realm: Recovering the Supernatural Worldview of the Bible*. (Lexham Press, 2015). 38.
[42] Ibid. 59.

and action to demonstrate that He never gives up on any diamond, no matter how lost or hidden. To Him, our value never changes."[43]

Additionally, looking at Imago Dei as a diamond prism, the prism still maintains its value even when it is covered with "stuff." All that is required is to be washed in the water of the word. When we do not know our identity, we operate in shame which causes the following manifestations: "withdrawal, shutting down, uncontrollable tears, anger, rage, self-pity, confusion, anxiety, defensiveness, or deep depression."[44] Mental health issues are attached to these manifestations.

The initials I.D. are an excellent acronym for our identity – **I**-mago **D**-ei. As in travelling, all persons must carry a valid government issued I.D. card to authenticate their identity. Our Imago Dei is identified by acknowledging the principles discussed here, and washing away the chocolate and candy coating of life's shame as Catherine Skurja has described.

Our identity is attached to the love of God. When there is a disconnection from this principle of love, an even more obvious disconnect occurs between the head and the heart of a person whose identity of God and the Imago Dei are distorted. It is at this point that mental health issues and physical illnesses manifest. Yet the bible instructs us to think on these things about ourselves, and others, see Philippians 4:8.

"Gregory of Nyssa, one of the early church writers termed the ongoing discovery of God as a journey of *'satisfied dissatisfaction.'* Every experience of God both completely

---

[43] Catherine Skurja. *Paradox Lost: Uncovering the True Identity in Christ.* (Imago Dei Resources LLC, 2012), 41.
[44] Ibid. 138.

satisfied him and increased his desire for more…which sent him seeking forever the deeper things of God."[45] Hence, the term *satisfied dissatisfaction* describes the God-addiction that believers who understand the Imago Dei will experience.

"The life-transforming power of God, the *satisfied dissatisfaction*, the healing of gaps between head and heart, is found in daily living these two great commandments: to love God with all that you are, and love your neighbor as yourself. All the brokenness and division of our lives and our world, *every* part of us, including the *stuck* parts, is to be brought together and focused on the same thing: **loving God**… A broken understanding of God and self will keep us from living out the first and second commandments."[46]

The love of God can be better identified by obtaining an understanding of ontology. "The difference between ontology [what a being is] and function [what a being does] is easily illustrated. The word 'human' is an ontological term. Humans [regardless of gender] can be doctors, lawyers, mechanics, engineers, and messengers. All those terms describe functions or tasks."[47] Functionally speaking, identity is not derived from anything on this list of what huMANkind does. Identity can only be formed ontologically, based on the fact that huMANkind are created in the image of the Community of God.

"We are God's representatives on earth. To *be* human is to image God. This is why Genesis 1:26-27 is followed by what theologians call the 'dominion mandate' in verse 28. The verse informs us that God intends us to be Him on this planet. We are to create more imagers

---

[45] Ibid. 4.
[46] Ibid. 17.
[47] Michael S. Heiser *The Unseen Realm: Recovering the Supernatural Worldview of the Bible*. (Lexham Press, 2015). 324.

['be fruitful and multiply…fill'] in order to oversee the earth by stewarding its resources and harnessing them for the benefit of all human imagers."[48]

HuMANkind are representatives of the Trinity for all of creation to engage. "Seeing the Trinity in Genesis 1:26 is reading the New Testament back into the Old Testament, something that isn't a sound interpretive method for discerning what an Old Testament writer was thinking…the triune godhead idea is never transparently expressed in the Old Testament."[49] Just as Jesus is concealed in the Old Testament, He is revealed in the New Testament as the Tree of Life to restore huMANkind to have continual access to the Trinity. "We are created in the image of God, and Jesus reconnects us to that reality. Our understanding of the Trinity and the Incarnation are key to our understanding of self and all relationships. Here is a summary of connections between triune God [Father, Son, Holy Spirit], Christ, and humankind: [50]

Triune God Is…	**Incarnate Christ Is…**	**We Are…**
…God.	…fully God, fully human.	…human beings created in the image of God.
…relational by nature.	…relational by nature.	…relational by nature.
…paradoxical by nature.	…paradoxical by nature.	…paradoxical by nature.
…Spirit.	…a spiritual being in a physical body.	…spiritual beings in physical bodies.
…love.	…love incarnate.	…created to love and be loved.

---

[48] Ibid. 43.
[49] Ibid. 23.
[50] Catherine Skurja. *Paradox Lost: Uncovering the True Identity in Christ*. (Imago Dei Resources LLC, 2012). 100.

"Each of us *needs* Jesus as Lord and Savior, NOT so that *we can* acquire an Imago Dei, but because *we must* surrender our lives to Him in order to uncover it."[51] This is the journey of a lifetime. We are "becoming individuals, realizing our own identity within, *so that* we can then relate creatively and positively to our family for the first time."[52]

Spirit

"Beyond the biological, psychological, and social aspects of our lives, we are also spiritual beings. To fully heal and be our best, it is important to recognize that we are more than just our bodies, minds, brains, and social connections."[53] We are created in the image of the spirit of God, therefore my spirit rejoices in God my Savior, see Luke 1:47. "It is imperative that a believer know he has a spirit, since, as we shall soon learn, every communication of God with man occurs there. If the believer does not discern his own spirit he invariably is ignorant of how to commune with God in the spirit. He easily substitutes the thoughts or emotions of the soul for the works of the spirit. Thus he confines himself to the outer realm, unable ever to reach the spiritual realm."[54] The following list of scriptures identifies the spirit:

- He who has no rule over his own spirit … Proverbs 25:28
- The Spirit Himself [thus] testifies together with our own spirit … Romans 8:16
- …to the spirits of the righteous … Hebrews 12:23

---

[51] Ibid. 44. Emphasis added.
[52] Sanford, John A. The Kingdom Within: The Inner Meaning of Jesus' Sayings. HarperOne, 1987. 61.
[53] Amen, Daniel G. *Change Your Brain, Change Your Life: The Breakthrough Program for Conquering Anxiety, Depression, Obsessiveness, Anger, and Impulsiveness*. (New York: Harmony, 2015). 53.
[54] Watchman Nee. *The Spiritual Man*. (New York: Christian Fellowship Publishers Inc, 1977). 31.

- … my spirit [by the Holy Spirit within me] prays … 1 Corinthians 14:14
- … the man's own spirit within … 1 Corinthians 2:11
- … forms the spirit of man within him … Zechariah 12:1

The bible reveals the human spirit as magnificent. Larry Crabb states: "From the moment of rebirth in Christ, every man and woman is made alive; alive *to* God, *for* God, and *with* God. God's spirit, the Spirit of relational holiness, lives in the center of every Christian woman, energizing her to relate in a way that reveals the invitational God who opens Himself to eagerly welcome all who hear His call and enter His community. That same Spirit makes His home in the center of every Christian man, empowering him to relate in a way that reveals the moving God who passionately longs to pour His life-giving love into every opened heart."[55]

John Loren and Paula Sanford have identified nine functions of the personal spirit in their book *God's Power To Change – healing the wounded* spirit:

1. Corporate worship
2. Private devotions
3. Hearing God
4. Inspiration
5. Transcending time
6. Communion and communication with others
7. Creating the glory of marital sexual union
8. Protection from disease and granting buoyancy in recovering quickly

---

[55] Larry Crabb. *Fully Alive: A Biblical Vision of Gender That Frees Men and Women to Live Beyond Stereotypes*. (Grand Rapids: Baker Books, 2013. Kindle edition). 159.

9. Providing a good conscience."[56]

There are many functions of the personal spirit, and scripture notes these different instances. Such as the fact that the sacrifice of a broken spirit which is pleasing to God, as the psalmists describes in Psalm 51:17. This is not referencing what is created in the Imago Dei. If a person's prism of Imago Dei, and personal spirit is broken, he or she could be more reliant on the incorrect spirit. What is more, the personal spirit can be wounded; and a person can have a slumbering spirit that needs to be awakened to living in God's light, see Ephesians 5:14.

The bible declares: "From now on, worshiping the Father will not be a matter of the right place but with a right heart. For God is a Spirit, and he longs to have sincere worshipers who adore him in the realm of the Spirit and in truth (John 4:23-24 TPT)." This text is commonly referred to in regards to worshipping the Father in spirit and in truth. We see the Passion Translation elaborates and exposes that the issue is about worshipping with a right heart in sincerity; the only way to access the spiritual realm of truth.

The Apostle Paul addresses a paradox that is essential to mental health and identity. It is a contrast between the natural man verses the spiritual man:

> Now we have not received the spirit [that belongs to] the world, but the [Holy] Spirit Who is from God, [given to us] that we might realize and comprehend and appreciate the gifts [of divine favor and blessing so freely and lavishly] bestowed on us by God. And we are setting these truths forth in words not taught by human wisdom but taught by the [Holy] Spirit, combining and interpreting spiritual truths with spiritual language [to those who possess the Holy Spirit]. But **the natural, nonspiritual man** does not accept or welcome or admit into his heart the gifts and teachings and revelations of the Spirit of God, for they are folly (meaningless nonsense) to him; and he is incapable of knowing them [of progressively recognizing, understanding, and becoming better acquainted with them] because they are spiritually discerned and estimated and

---
[56] John L. Sandford, and Paula Sandford. *Healing the Wounded Spirit*. (Victory House Publishers, 1985).28-29.

appreciated. But **the spiritual man** tries all things [he examines, investigates, inquires into, questions, and discerns all things], yet is himself to be put on trial and judged by no one [he can read the meaning of everything, but no one can properly discern or appraise or get an insight into him] (1 Corinthians 2:12-15 AMPC, emphasis added).

Pastor Paul Trulin explains that "the **natural man's** relationship is with the world, sin and Satan … All of his existence is centered on himself … and he has no spiritual values, but walks in utter darkness … The natural man has no knowledge of God. He is in fact an enemy of God and has no love for Him."[57] Regarding the spiritual man Trulin offers that "the spiritual man not only has received Christ as his Savior, but he also made Him the sole Master of his life… in opposition to the natural man, the spiritual man's only motivation is Jesus Christ. In worldly colloquialism: he sleeps, eats, drinks, breathes and talks Jesus Christ. Everything he does for Christ is out of love. He detests the world, sin, and the devil. In fact, he reckons himself dead to these."[58]

We will revisit this principle in the latter part of the research. Suffice it for now that the spiritual man must progressively mature once born again. He must matriculate through the stages of the carnal natural man, to a babe in Christ, and finally to a mature son of God.

Soul

In the book *Renewal of the Mind! According to Romans 12:1-3* the author has a chapter titled *Battlefield*. The first topic in this chapter is *This Is Not A Battle, This is War*, which exposes the battlefield of the mind and the role of grace on the battlefield. Additionally, this chapter identifies the enemy and the warfare in the thought life of believers. She concludes

---

[57] Paul G. Trulin. *My Body, His Life*, 11th ed. (Sacramento: Paul Trulin Ministries, 1989).75.
[58] Ibid. 76.

this chapter delineating between the heart and soul, discussing the future glory that is to be revealed through those who have renewed their mind, and concludes the chapter exposing deception – which is another Screwtape Element. To quote some of this concept: "We are exposing the tactics, plans, strategies of the enemy on the battleground of the mind — which is the soulish realm: the mind, will, emotion, imagination, intellect, reasoning, thoughts, personality; conscious, memory. This is the battlefield — and if the enemy can mess up your thinking, he can have you living raggedy. But the Lord is exposing and revealing the plans, tactics, strategies of the enemy."[59]

Another strategy of deception is to cause believers to misunderstand what is being referred to when someone says soul. Francis Frangipane states that "most of us understand the basic dynamics of the human soul…in addition to the mind, the will and the emotions, the soul is made of events and how we responded to those events… Our reaction to each event, whether that event was positive or negative, is poured into the creative marrow of our individuality, where it is blended into the nature of our character. What we call *memory* is actually our spirit gazing at the substance of our soul… for although the events of our lives are irreversible, our reactions to those events can still be changed."[60]

Several authors discussed the principle of the formation of identity in early childhood. "Each child is born in the image of the fallen Adam with a spirit of bondage to fear (Hebrews 2:15 and Romans 8:15)."[61] In her book *Critical Spirit: Confronting the Heart of a Critic*, June Hunt discusses the: "Five States of Childhood Development: God bestows on parents the

---

[59] Paulette Denise. *Renewal of the Mind! According to Romans 12:2*. (A Portion Ministries, 2014). 53.
[60] Francis Frangipane. *The Three Battlegrounds: An In-Depth View of the Three Arenas of Spiritual Warfare: the Mind, the Church and the Heavenly Places*, 2nd ed. (Cedar Rapids: Arrow Publications, 2010). 92.
[61] William G. Null. *Rejection - Its Fruits and Its Roots: A Scriptural Understanding of Rejection, How it Works and How to Minister*. (Impact Christian Books Inc, Kirkwood, MO, 2005). 241.

major responsibility of nurturing their children so that they will not be *love-starved* – an emotional state that sets them up to 'look for love in all the wrong places.'

1) The helpless stage; as babies.

2) The pushing away stage; as toddlers.

3) The conflict stage; as young children.

4) The independent stage; as preadolescent children.

5) The sharing stage; as adolescents."[62]

Hunt goes on to recite that "in reality, we have all been created with three God-given inner needs; the needs of love, significance, and security."[63] These inner needs are of the soul and are to be met by the Ultimate Need-Meeter, whom we are created in the image of.

The thought life is maintained in the soul. Both Dr. Caroline Leaf and Dr. Daniel Amen deliberated about the thought life in several of their books. "Toxic thinking is essentially a roadblock in the *Perfect You*. If these negative thought patterns are not controlled, they can even lead to psychiatric symptoms including depression, anxiety, suicidal ideation, OCD, eating disorders, and psychotic breaks."[64]

In his book, *Change Your Brain, Change Your Life, Dr*. Daniel Amen describes an acronym he coined in the 1990s ANT Therapy to address the **A**utomatic **N**egative **T**houghts that must be addressed to create and sustain a healthy psychological limbic system. The Amen Clinics assists clients and encourage them that "Truly learning these principles will help you

---

[62] June Hunt. *Critical Spirit: Confronting the Heart of a Critic*, 7th ed. (Peabody, MA:-Hendrickson Publishers, 2017). 36-37.
[63] Ibid. 44.
[64] Leaf, Caroline. The Perfect You: A Blueprint for Identity. Ada: Baker Books, 2017. 80.

gain more control over your feelings and behavior."⁶⁵ The following list summarizes the different ANT types identified:

1. All-or-nothing thinking: thoughts that things are all good or all bad.
2. 'Always' thinking: thinking in words like *always, never, no one, everyone, every time, or everything*.
3. Focusing on the negative: only seeing the bad in a situation.
4. Fortune telling: predicting the worst possible outcome to a situation with little or no evidence for it.
5. Mind reading: believing that you know what another person is thinking even though they haven't told you.
6. Thinking with your feelings: believing negative feelings without ever questioning them.
7. Guilt beatings: thinking in words like *should, must, ought, or have to*.
8. Labeling: attaching a negative label to yourself or to someone else.
9. Blaming: blaming someone else for the problems you have.

   Your thoughts matter. Kill the ANTs and train your thoughts to be positive and it will benefit your mind, mood, and body.⁶⁶

The soul prospers in understanding it's identity in the spirit realm: which is a progressive revelation due to the renewing of the mind. "Beloved, I pray that **you** may prosper in every way and [that your **body**] may keep well, even as [I know] your **soul** keeps well and prospers (3 John 2 AMPC, emphasis added)." Regarding the body keeping well, a noted healing element to bring balance with mental health issues is to take into account somatic experiencing which addresses trauma in the nervous system during the formative times of identity. Somatic, means body, and things have happened to the body which have caused an impairment in the soul, thus hindering the ability to truly grasp the fact that the spirit is created in the image of God, which is true identity, the concept and principle of the image of God, the Imago Dei, the diamond that is covered with the cares and concerns of the world.

---

⁶⁵ Amen, Daniel G. *Change Your Brain, Change Your Life: The Breakthrough Program for Conquering Anxiety, Depression, Obsessiveness, Anger, and Impulsiveness.* (New York: Harmony, 2015). 109.
⁶⁶ Ibid. 116-117.

<u>Body</u>

One way in which mental health issues manifests is when a person's only identity is his or her body. This is conjectural because mental health originates in between the dimensions of the body and the soul. Hence if a person derives their identity from either the body or the soul, instead of the spirit which is created in the image of God, mental health issues may manifest. In this section we will briefly acquire an understanding of the scientific working of the brain which will assist in addressing symptoms that manifest. Scientifically speaking, "a fetus could be said to develop from the inside, or brain, out. First to take recognizable shape in the womb is an embryonic central nervous system – later to become the brain and spinal cord – and around this core the rest of the body forms … The brain reaches between 75 to 80 percent of adult size within the first two years … Neurons are widely spaced at birth, but immediately, connections begin to form."[67]

There is a vast difference between the brain and the mind. Dr. Daniel G. Amen and Dr. Caroline Leaf provide foundational insights as to the connection of the brain, which is the body, and the soul, which is where mental health issues manifest which will be discussed in depth in chapter four. For this section, we will look at a simplified explanation of the brain from the profound book titled *Scared Sick*:

> Brain development basically occurs from the bottom up. The first part of the brain to develop is the most primitive: the *brain stem* controls the most basic functions of the body over which we have no conscious control, like blood pressure, body temperature and respiration. Next comes the *midbrain*, which controls bodily functions over which we have some awareness and control, like appetite and sleep. Then the *limbic brain* develops: this is the seat of emotion and impulse. Finally, developing the most slowly, is the *cortex*, the outside layer of the brain that is the seat of logic, planning and rational

---

[67] Reader's Digest. *ABC's of the Human Mind: A Family Answer Book.* (New York: Readers Digest, 1990). 64.

thought, and the 'executive functions.' It is worth noting that complex cortical skills, such as self-control and connecting what we do today with what may happen a week from Friday, are still very much coming online throughout adolescence – which is why so many teenagers have such difficulty with these capacities.[68]

Frontal Lobe	Temporal Lobe	Occipital Lobe	Parietal Lobe
Just behind and above the eyes **Prefrontal Cortex:** reasoning, planning, emotions **Broca's Area:** controls muscles that produce speech **Premotor Cortex:** skilled coordination involving many muscles **Motor Cortex:** controls voluntary muscles **Supplementary Motor Area:**	At the temple **Wernicke's Area:** understanding speech and other sensory information. Hearing. Connected to the limbic system, affects emotions	Lower back and base of the skull **Somatosensory Cortex:** receives and interprets signals from all senses **Vision Centers:** receiving and interpreting visual signals	Back top half and sides of the skull; rear of frontal lobes **Somatosensory Cortex:** receives and interprets signals from all senses

[69]

The above adaptation of the workings of the four lobes of the brain is a quick reference for understanding the functions of the lobes. The hypothalamus is sometimes labeled the 'brain within the brain,' or the power behind the endocrine system. The preceding briefly summarizes the endocrine system: "Hypothalamus governs the endocrine system, using the pituitary as an intermediary. Pituitary gland stimulates bone growth, regulates sexual development, and the activity of other glands. Thyroid gland controls the rate of metabolism. Pineal gland may have a role in sexual development and menstruation. Parathyroid gland controls the level of calcium in the blood. Also the thymus, adrenals, pancreas, and ovaries or testes are other major endocrine glands."[70]

---

[68] Robin Karr-Morse, and Meredith S. Wiley. *Scared Sick: The Role of Childhood Trauma in Adult Disease.* (New York, Basic Books, 2012). 98.
[69] Reader's Digest. *ABC's of the Human Mind: A Family Answer Book.* (New York: Readers Digest, 1990). 73.
[70] Ibid. 76.

The following are examples of issues with the body that some people do not realize, and misappropriate as identity, or identify with improperly:

- The release of hormones cannot be felt physically.

- "When the basal ganglia are overactive ... people are more likely to be overwhelmed by stressful situations and have a tendency to freeze or become immobile (in thoughts or actions)."[71]

- "The central difference between toxic stress and trauma is that *trauma always triggers the freeze response*. When we are unable to fight or flee, freezing is the only option left."[72]

- "When the limbic system is overactive, people tend toward depression, negativity, and distancing themselves from others ... They tend to push people away with their negativity."[73]

- "The two parts of the brain, the limbic system and pre-frontal cortex, are split from one another when we are having a shame reaction... When shame is triggered, the limbic system will win out every time."[74]

These issues will be discussed in part two of this research. Conversely, apprehension of the Community of God, as well as the tri-part being of huMANkind and the Imago Dei

---

[71] Amen, Daniel G. *Change Your Brain, Change Your Life: The Breakthrough Program for Conquering Anxiety, Depression, Obsessiveness, Anger, and Impulsiveness*. (New York: Harmony, 2015). 133.
[72] Robin Karr-Morse, and Meredith S. Wiley. *Scared Sick: The Role of Childhood Trauma in Adult Disease*. (New York, Basic Books, 2012). 24-25.
[73] Amen, Daniel G. *Change Your Brain, Change Your Life: The Breakthrough Program for Conquering Anxiety, Depression, Obsessiveness, Anger, and Impulsiveness*. (New York: Harmony, 2015). 298.
[74] Catherine Skurja. *Paradox Lost: Uncovering the True Identity in Christ*. (Imago Dei Resources LLC, 2012). 237.

are required for sound identity. The following chapter will expose an element that hinders believers from discovering and fulfilling identity.

CHAPTER THREE: Screwtape Element

"And from the days of John the Baptist until now the kingdom of heaven has been treated violently, and violent men take it by force (Matthew 11:12 NASB)." I found this scripture to be indirectly and factiously explained in the book *The Screwtape Letters* by C.S. Lewis. "The commonest question is whether I really 'believe in the Devil.' Now, if by 'the Devil' you mean a power opposite to God and, like God, self-existent from all eternity, the answer is certainly NO. There is no uncreated being except God. God has no opposite … The proper question is whether I believe in devils. I do. That is to say, I believe in angels, and I believe that some of these, by the abuse of their free will, have become enemies to God and, as a corollary, to us. These we may call devils. They do not differ in nature from good angels, but their nature is depraved. *Devil* is opposite of *angel* only as Bad Man is the opposite of Good Man. Satan, the leader or dictator of devils, is the opposite, not of God, but of Michael."[75]

My summary of the Screwtape Element (as I have coined) is to get huMANkind, especially believers who have not thoroughly understood their Imago Dei, to focus more on surface issues, and anything other than living as an upright citizen of the kingdom of God. Hence, the kingdom suffers violence. Unsurprisingly, this is probably why there is such a great assault on children? As we will discuss in PART TWO of this project, the enemy uses Adverse Childhood Experiences (ACEs) and traumatic events to distort identity because personality and personhood are usually formed by the age of 6 years old.

---

[75] Clive S. Lewis. *The Screwtape Letters; With, Screwtape Proposes a Toast*. (Scribner Paper Fiction, 1982). vii.

Lewis goes on to describe: "My symbol for Hell is something like the bureaucracy of a police state or the offices of a thoroughly nasty business ... Here again my symbol seemed to me useful. It enables me, by earthly parallels, to picture an official society held together entirely by fear and greed. On the surface, manners are normally suave. Rudeness to one's superiors would obviously be suicidal; rudeness to one's equals might put them on their guard before you were ready to spring your mine ... Everyone wishes everyone else's discrediting, demotion, and ruin; and everyone is an expert in the confidential report, the pretended alliance, the stab in the back."[76]

In the Screwtape account of the violent, but non-violent attacks on the kingdom, the focus is intentionally skewed from relationship with the Holy Trinity, or even acknowledging the inherent Imago Dei. Another ditch of focus is on the fall of huMANkind, and other theological debates. However, in the book *The Kingdom Within*, John A. Sanford states: "In dwelling exclusively on the Fall, on the need to be obedient to God and be restored from our fallen state to a sort of blamelessness, traditional theology has missed the significance of the kingdom of God. For the kingdom is not obedience, but creativity; it is not restoration to a former primitive state from which we fell, but is reunification on a much higher level."[77]

An alternative strategy of Satan is to counterfeit everything that God has. R.B. Thieme Jr. labels Satan as a master counterfeiter who masquerades as an angel of light. "He is a master of deceit. Were he visible today, millions would be captivated by his charming personality and deny that he is evil. Why is the devil so intent on revealing himself in the best possible light? To seduce as many followers away from Jesus Christ as possible, ever seeking to avert

---

[76] Ibid. x-xi.
[77] Sanford, John A. The Kingdom Within: The Inner Meaning of Jesus' Sayings. HarperOne, 1987. 66.

his inevitable doom. One of Satan's greatest stratagems has been the attempt to keep men in ignorance of the real nature of his being and the fraudulent dimensions of his pretensions."[78] Scripture describes this agenda in John 8:44 when it describes the enemy as the father of lies who speaks falsehood. He has inundated the world with multiple counterfeit doctrines:

> **Counterfeit 'false' teachers and prophets**
> 2 Corinthians 11:13-15; Isaiah 41:29; Matthew 7:15, 24:24; 2 Peter 2:1; 1 John 4:1
> **Counterfeit 'false' communion table**
> 1 Corinthians 10:21
> **Counterfeit 'false' righteousness**
> Matthew 19:16-26, Isaiah 64:6
> **Counterfeit 'false' gospel or Jesus**
> 2 Corinthians 11:3-4
> **Counterfeit 'false' salvation based on works**
> Galatians 2:2-3
> **Counterfeit 'false' personality and outer masks (Pharisaical hypocrisy)**
> Luke 13:15-16
> **Counterfeit 'false' religions**
> 1 Samuel 15:23; Acts 25:19; Colossians 2:23; 2 Timothy 3:5
> **Counterfeit 'false' femininity and masculinity**
> Esther 1:1-12, Romans 1:26-27
> **Counterfeit 'false' repentance (shallow, superficial repentance)**
> Matthew 23:27, Luke 3:7-14, Mark 7:6
> **Counterfeit 'false' discernment**
> John 5:30, 7:24; Philippians 1:9

These counterfeits can manifest in varying ways that many people wouldn't even recognize as counterfeits, or idols. Yet Catherine Skurja says "anything or anyone that comes between God and me is an idol and keeps me from abiding in my Imago Dei … Whenever we make judgments and create idols, we are outside our Imago Dei, functioning under the Fall."[79]

---

[78] R. B. Thieme, Jr. *Satan and Demonism, 3rd ed.* (Houston, TX: R. B. Thieme, Jr., Bible Ministries, 1996). 5.
[79] Catherine Skurja. *Paradox Lost: Uncovering the True Identity in Christ.* (Imago Dei Resources LLC, 2012). 164-165.

All of this is part of the violent battle for righteousness and authentic worship. John MacArthur lists four kinds of worship that are unacceptable to God, and are viewed as idolatry:

1. "The worship of false gods, see Job 31:24-28.
2. The worship of the true God in a wrong form, see Exodus 32:7-9.
3. The worship of the true God in a self-styled manner, see Matthew 15:3.
4. The worship of the true God in the right way, with a wrong attitude, see Isaiah 1:11-15."[80]

Again, the focus is worship, counterfeited by idolatry unawares. "Now it is not enough to note that there is no question in Jesus' mind that the kingdom of Satan is not divided against itself. Evil is single in its intention, and this intention is to destroy wholeness. Evil is anti-wholeness, and therefore is opposed to God's kingdom. As long as human beings are inwardly in conflict, divided within themselves, victims of their own inner opposition, they are easy prey for evil. But where the kingdom of God is being established in an individual, that person is also becoming whole and the kingdom of evil has no power over him or her."[81]

One of the Screwtape Elements is the enemy's desire to distort the identity of huMANkind and to cause mankind to think that distorted identity is acceptable. When in reality, "we bear the image of a relational God, the Trinity. To be truly formed like Jesus means to relate like Jesus. Spiritual formation is a relational formation."[82] Not only personal spiritual formation, but collectively as a church. "This is exactly what the warfare is centered

---

[80] John F. MacArthur *Worship: The Ultimate Priority*. (Chicago: Moody Publishers, 2012). 22-25.
[81] Sanford, John A. The Kingdom Within: The Inner Meaning of Jesus' Sayings. HarperOne, 1987. 40.
[82] Larry Crabb. *Fully Alive: A Biblical Vision of Gender That Frees Men and Women to Live Beyond Stereotypes*. (Grand Rapids: Baker Books, 2013. Kindle edition)., 27.

upon in the church today: the devil wants us to accept Christianity as it is, as though division, sin, and spiritual impotency were the ultimate reality God has provided for believers on earth. Satan wants us to *agree with and thereby reinforce* this deceptive view of the church."[83]

Subtly is a cloak the enemy uses to work the Screwtape Element. "In the Church Age Satan is far too subtle to tempt Christians with such horrors as child sacrifice. Instead, he distracts the believer from the plan of God by appealing to the 'lust of the flesh, lust of the eyes, and the boastful pride of life' as in 1 John 2:16. Succumbing to these seductive lusts carries a high price for the believer."[84] Something else the adversary uses to entrap believers is to suggest the following: "Focusing only on changing sinful behavior fails to take into account the need for shame to be healed from the very root so the HEART can change."[85] All the while masking the true change needed in the heart.

Focusing only on sinful behaviors is an attempt to function with a mask on, or as the biblical term, as a hypocrite. "There is a certain usefulness to this outer mask, for to some extent we need to function in the world. The destructive aspect of the mask is our tendency to identify with it, to think that we are the person we pretend to be, and thereby to remain unconscious of our real self … On the other hand, to persist in identifying with the mask is to foster a split within ourselves. Then the house of our soul is divided against itself and cannot stand."[86]

---

[83] Francis Frangipane. *The Three Battlegrounds: An In-Depth View of the Three Arenas of Spiritual Warfare: the Mind, the Church and the Heavenly Places*, 2nd ed. (Cedar Rapids: Arrow Publications, 2010). 109.
[84] R. B. Thieme, Jr. *Satan and Demonism, 3rd ed.* (Houston, TX: R. B. Thieme, Jr., Bible Ministries, 1996). 9.
[85] Catherine Skurja. *Paradox Lost: Uncovering the True Identity in Christ*. (Imago Dei Resources LLC, 2012). 119.
[86] Sanford, John A. The Kingdom Within: The Inner Meaning of Jesus' Sayings. HarperOne, 1987. 70, 79.

An element of Screwtape occurs when the enemy insights people to fight over the paradox of 'either/or' and 'neither/both'. Catherine Skurja depicts this conflict as such: "When we endeavor to hold the tension of paradox, we find freedom from the confinement of our compartmentalized thinking. As we taste and see that God is good and that He loves us, we escape the confines of 'either/or' and can accept that the mysteries of life and God will not be resolved to fit into all our little mental boxes. Our view of God begins to allow for paradoxical tension, and our head and heart begin to come into unity and agreement."[87] Therefore, the enemy uses his age-old weapon of religion to keep believers on the surface level of understanding, and never dive deeper into the meaning of paradoxes and parables.

John A. Sanford quoted "Fritz Kunkel in these words: 'Religion, without a thorough study of sin, religion without awareness of conscious and unconscious, individual and collective darkness, evil and deviation, is not religion but blind idolatry … This means that as long as we are not whole we are always more or less a prey to evil, and out of this arises a host of symptoms."[88] Michael Heiser adds that "evil is the perversion of God's good gift of free will. It arises from the choices made by imperfect imagers, not from God's prompting or predestination. God does not need evil, but He has the power to take the evil that flows from free-will-decisions – human or otherwise – and use it to produce good and His glory through the obedience of His loyal imagers, who are His hands and feet on the ground now."[89]

We will continue to examine these Screwtape Elements throughout the remainder of part two of this project. The bible speaks extensively to alert believers regarding the plans of

---

[87] Catherine Skurja. *Paradox Lost: Uncovering the True Identity in Christ*. (Imago Dei Resources LLC, 2012). 21.
[88] Sanford, John A. The Kingdom Within: The Inner Meaning of Jesus' Sayings. HarperOne, 1987. 105.
[89] Michael S. Heiser *The Unseen Realm: Recovering the Supernatural Worldview of the Bible*. (Lexham Press, 2015). 66.

the enemy in Job 10:3; Psalm 10:2, 140:1; Isaiah 29:15, 32:7; and 2 Corinthians 2:10-11. "So that we would not be exploited by the adversary, Satan, for we know his clever schemes (2 Corinthians 2:11 TPT)."

PART TWO: DICHOTOMY OF MENTAL HEALTH
CHAPTER FOUR: Mental Health

Mental health is not a disease and should not be looked at the same as say diabetes, heart maladies, or a broken arm. Those are conditions that physical tests can diagnose, and medication can be prescribed to manage and heal. However, mental health cannot be fully measured with an x-ray or CAT scan because it is not biological or something that can be seen in the physical body. "Mental health is defined as a state of well-being in which every individual realizes his or her own potential, can cope with the normal stresses of life, can work productively and fruitfully, and is able to make a contribution to his or her community."[90] The following statistics show that there is a growing concern for mental health:

Statistics

- "Mental illnesses are common in the United States. Nearly one in five U.S. adults live with a mental illness (51.5 million in 2019). Mental illnesses include many different conditions that vary in degree of severity, ranging from mild to, moderate to severe.
- An estimated 49.5% of adolescents had any mental disorder.
- Of adolescents with any mental disorder, an estimated 22.2% had severe impairment. DSM-IV based criteria were used to determine impairment level."[91]

---

[90] Leaf, Caroline. The Perfect You: A Blueprint for Identity. Ada: Baker Books, 2017.

[91] "NIMH Mental Illness." (NIMH Home. Accessed April 26, 2021).

- "Twenty-six percent of adults over eighteen suffer from a diagnosable mental disorder. Eighteen percent of adults in the United States over age eighteen suffer from an anxiety disorder."[92]

These statistics are staggering! This section will delve deeper into understanding the roots of mental health issues in an effort to identify and assist people through to wholeness. As will be discussed a little further in this chapter, there are several causes for these manifestations of mental health issues. In her book *The Perfect You*, Dr. Caroline Leaf notes that: "It is trauma and habitual incorrect thought reactions that have not been dealt with, where we have stepped out of our *Perfect You* in response to the events and circumstances of our lives. This creates neurological chaos that can manifest as disorders of the mind, with concomitant symptoms erroneously termed biological diseases."[93]

Most mental health disorders can be viewed as a lack of wisdom in response to life as a result of faulty identity foundations. The bible describes the double-minded response like this: "If any of you is deficient in wisdom, let him ask of the giving God [Who gives] to everyone liberally and ungrudgingly, without reproaching or faultfinding, and it will be given him. Only it must be in faith that he asks with no wavering (no hesitating, no doubting). For the one who wavers (hesitates, doubts) is like the billowing surge out at sea that is blown hither and thither and tossed by the wind. For truly, let not such a person imagine that he will receive anything [he asks for] from the Lord, [For being as he is] a man of two minds (hesitating, dubious, irresolute), [he is] unstable and unreliable and uncertain about everything

---

[92] Robin Karr-Morse, and Meredith S. Wiley. *Scared Sick: The Role of Childhood Trauma in Adult Disease*. (New York, Basic Books, 2012). xiv.
[93] Leaf, Caroline. The Perfect You: A Blueprint for Identity. Ada: Baker Books, 2017. 56.

[he thinks, feels, decides] (James 1:5-8 AMPC)." Other versions of the bible describe this as "a double-minded" person, who is unstable in all of their ways.

Arthur Null adds that "if we doubt God's promise, then we allow fear and pride to drive us like a wave on the sea. It is the doubt that causes us to not receive from the Lord... In Philippians 4:6-7 the Apostle Paul teaches the people to make their request known to God in everything, every circumstance – by prayer and humble petitions, with thanksgiving. This dispels anxiety and protects our hearts and minds, because we receive God's peace and wisdom as we choose to trust Him and stop leaning on our own understanding (our own soulish wisdom)."[94] The soul must be renewed to the identity in the Imago Dei. If not, mental health issues may manifest. The following is a list of common mental health issues discovered throughout this research project:

- Depression
- Anxiety/Worry
- ADD/ADHD
- Narcissistic Behavior
- Addictive Behavior
- Codependency
- Major Mental Disorders (see inserted table on the next page from Dr. Gary Collins)."[95]

This list is comparative to the list from the Reader's Digest book on the *ABCs of the Human Mind* which describes these as disorders of the mind that the American Psychiatric

---

[94] William G. Null. *Rejection - Its Fruits and Its Roots: A Scriptural Understanding of Rejection, How it Works and How to Minister*. (Impact Christian Books Inc, Kirkwood, MO, 2005). 247.
[95] Gary R. Collins. *Christian Counseling: A Comprehensive Guide*. (W Publishing Group, 1988). 471.

Association has divided into categories and began "publishing diagnostic guidelines in the 1950s known as the Diagnostic and Statistical Manual of Mental Disorders DSM-III-R."[96]

---

[96] Reader's Digest. *ABC's of the Human Mind: A Family Answer Book*. (New York: Readers Digest, 1990). 40.

1) Disorders Usually First Evident in Infancy, Childhood, or Adolescence
    - Disruptive Behavior Disorders
    - Anxiety Disorders of Childhood Adolescence
    - Eating Disorders
    - Gender Identity Disorders
    - Tic Disorders
    - Elimination Disorders
    - Speech Disorders Not Elsewhere Classified
    - Other Disorders of Infancy, Childhood or Adolescence
2) Organic Mental Syndromes and Disorders
    - Dementias Arising in the Senium and Presenium (This includes Alzheimer's Disease and Senile Dementia)
3) Psychoactive Substance Abuse Disorders
    - This includes dependence and abuse of alcohol, caffeine, cocaine, hallucinogens, inhalants, nicotine, sedatives and other substances
4) Schizophrenia
    - This includes catatonic, disorganized, paranoid, undifferentiated and residual types.
5) Delusional (Paranoid) Disorders
    - This includes erotomanic, grandiose, jealous, persecutory, somatic and unspecified types.
6) Psychotic Disorders Not Elsewhere Classified
7) Mood Disorders
    - Bipolar Disorders (including mixed manic-depressive and manic disorders)
    - Depressive Disorders
8) Anxiety disorders
    - This includes panic disorders, phobias, obsessive-compulsive disorders, and post-traumatic disorders.
9) Somatoform Disorders
    - These are disorders concerning the body including hypochondriasis and conversion disorders.
10) Dissociative Disorders
    - These include multiple personality disorder, psychogenic amnesia, and depersonalization disorder.
11) Sexual Disorders
    - Paraphilias (including exhibitionism, fetishism, predophilia, sexual masochism, sexual sadism, transvestism, and voyeurism)
    - Sexual Dysfunctions (including hypoactive sexual desire, sexual aversion, sexual arousal disorders, orgasm disorders and sexual pain disorders)
12) Sleep Disorders
    - These include insomnia, disorders in the sleep-wake schedule, nightmares, sleep terror disorder, sleepwalking and parasomnia.
13) Factitious Disorders
    - These are disorders in which physical and psychological symptoms are feigned.
14) Impulsive Disorders Not Elsewhere Classified
    - These include kleptomania, pathological gambling, pyromania and impulse control disorders.
15) Adjustment Disorders
    - Includes adjustment difficulties associated with
        - anxious mood
        - depressed mood
        - disturbance of conduct
        - physical complaints
        - withdrawal
        - work or academic inhibition
16) Psychological Factors Affecting Physical Condition
17) Personality Disorders
    - These include paranoid, schizoid, antisocial, borderline, and narcissistic personalities.
18) Conditions Not Attributable to a Mental Disorder but the Focus of Attention or Treatment
    - Academic Problem
    - Antisocial Problem
    - Malingering
    - Marital Problem
    - Noncompliance with Medical Treatment
    - Occupational Problem
    - Parent-child Problem
    - Other Interpersonal Problem
    - Other Specified Family Circumstances
    - Phase of Life Problem or Other Life Circumstance
    - Uncomplicated Bereavement

Centuries of mental illness and disorders have been a difficult matter to comprehend. "In 1883, at the age of 27, the German psychiatrist Emil Kraepelin began publishing a classification of mental illnesses. He created categories based on the onset, symptoms, development, and outcome of an illness."[97] Several additions have been made to this growing list over the decades.

Psychology describes and chronicles the deceits of the flesh. Yet Jesus overcomes the flesh. The word *psychology* means 'the study of the soul' and *psychiatry* means 'the healing of the soul.' John A. Sanford noted that "psychology, for the most part, proved itself also to be handmaiden of rationalism and materialism."[98] Both rationalism and materialism are at the crux of mental health issues.

The Reader's Digest Association posed the following question and response: "Is psychology really a science? Although most scientists do not deny that 'talk therapy' on the Freudian model has helped many people, it bothers some scientists that nobody can say for sure how or why it works, after almost a century of use. One philosopher, Patricia Churchland of the University of California at San Diego, has pointed out that the portion of the brain reachable by talk – our conscious, thinking, introspective self – is 'only a little bubble of froth,' beneath which the huge preponderance of brain activity proceeds, in effect, on its own. Thus, suggests Harvard University psychologist Howard Gardner, the classic introspective dimension of psychology, dealing with such questions as character and motivation, is really closer to cultural studies and the issues addressed in great literature."[99]

---

[97] Reader's Digest. *ABC's of the Human Mind: A Family Answer Book*. (New York: Readers Digest, 1990). 35.
[98] Sanford, John A. The Kingdom Within: The Inner Meaning of Jesus' Sayings. HarperOne, 1987. 119.
[99] Reader's Digest. *ABC's of the Human Mind: A Family Answer Book*. (New York: Readers Digest, 1990). 19.

In addition, Reader's Digest provided the following list of the wide variety of therapies now available: psychoanalysis; brief dynamic psychotherapy; behavior therapy; cognitive therapy, Rogerian therapy; Gestalt therapy; group therapy; hypnotherapy; and play therapy.[100] The three that I most identify with in my personal counseling style are cognitive, Rogerian, and group therapy.

"To truly transform our understanding of mental illnesses, we need to start by characterizing all cell types in the nervous system, and further identify their roles in the myriad aspects of mental processes… Through basic science, researchers endeavor to answer fundamental questions about the mechanisms (e.g. brain, behavioral, environmental, psychosocial) that contribute to cognition, perception, motivation, and social behavior. We have seen extraordinary progress in basic science over the past several years, including in neuroscience."[101] Examining neuroscience in the context of mental illness is a doorway to mental wholeness and health.

Identity Crisis

Mental health issues can be described as an identity crisis. As described in the earlier chapters about understanding the identity of the Community of God; recognizing that God has created huMANkind as male and female; understanding the realms of spirit, soul, body, and the Imago Dei of mankind; along with the identified Screwtape Elements – all of these things can create identity crises. We will now delve even deeper into understanding the

---

[100] Reader's Digest. *ABC's of the Human Mind: A Family Answer Book*. (New York: Readers Digest, 1990). 35.
[101] "NIMH Mental Illness." (NIMH Home. Accessed April 26, 2021).

manifestations of identity crisis. The previously discussed statistics are staggering, as well as the lists of identified mental disorders that have been compiled over the years. It is interesting that counselors, and church leaders have not connected these identity crises.

This portion of the research will now expose the identity crises of lost, stolen, suppressed, or unrealized identity as a result of the carnal nature, distorted identity through fear, rebellion, rejection, trauma, and adverse childhood experiences ACEs. All of these can cause a person to have a critical spirit and be prone to be codependent. The following rather large insert from the manual *Rejection - Its Fruits and Its Roots: A Scriptural Understanding of Rejection, How it Works and How to Minister,* illustrates the genesis of this crisis in the bible, and in huMANkind:

> Adam and Eve begot many children. Scripture tells us that we are descended from their son, Seth (Genesis 5:3), from whose line Noah descended. Because of this, we can see that we are begotten in the image and likeness of fallen Adam with his fallen, rebellious nature (Ephesians 2:1-3), separated from God and in bondage to sin which dwells in our bodies. The result of Eve's belief in deception (that God had rejected them from being completely like Him), brought in rebellion – rejection of God's commandment by her, and her mate. Although Adam had not been deceived, he willingly partook of something forbidden. For both Adam and Eve, this brought spiritual death and separation from God and His love. Their first response to this was to realize that their covering or protection was gone, and they reacted in pride by attempting to make their own covering. Secondly, they hid themselves from God, because they were afraid. The results of rejection coming into man are seen as fear on one hand, and pride (or self-fulfillment) on the other. Pride sent forth rebellion and the projection of blame onto someone else.[102]

As depicted earlier in the section identifying the spirit of man when we contrasted the natural and spiritual man (1 Corinthians 2:12-15), another identity crisis is for huMANkind to operate from the carnal nature.

---

[102] William G. Null. *Rejection - Its Fruits and Its Roots: A Scriptural Understanding of Rejection, How it Works and How to Minister.* (Impact Christian Books Inc, Kirkwood, MO, 2005). 26-27.

Carnal Nature

The carnal nature focuses on external things, and the things of this world. "For all that is in the world—the **lust of the flesh** [*craving for sensual gratification*] and the **lust of the eyes** [*greedy longings of the mind*] and the **pride of life** [*assurance in one's own resources or in the stability of earthly things*]—these do not come from the Father but are from the world [itself] (1 John 2:16 AMPC, emphasis added)." The carnal mind is dominated by lust. The following list are manifestations of the carnal mind (fleshly responses) compiled from the AMPC version of Ephesians 4:29-31, Colossians 3:5-9, and Galatians 5:19-21. If these things are present and evident in a person's history, they may open the door to mental health issues.

Immorality	Selfishness	Covetousness
Impurity	Divisions (dissensions)	Rage
Indecency	Envy	Anger (ill temper)
Idolatry	Drunkenness	Bad feelings toward others
Sorcery	Carousing	Curses
Enmity	Sexual vice	Slander
Strife	Sensual appetites	Greed
Jealousy	Unholy desires	Lying to one another
Party spirit (factions, sects with peculiar opinions, heresies)	Foulmouthed abuse and shameful utterances	

Spiritual growth is required to press out of carnality and these evident practices of the flesh and carnal nature. "Now the doings (practices) of the flesh are clear (obvious): they are ... I warn you beforehand, just as I did previously, that those who do such things shall not inherit the kingdom of God. But **the fruit of the [Holy] Spirit [the work which His presence**

within accomplishes] is love, joy (gladness), peace, patience (an even temper, forbearance), kindness, goodness (benevolence), faithfulness, gentleness (meekness, humility), self-control (self-restraint, continence). Against such things there is no law [that can bring a charge] (Galatians 5:19a, 22-23 AMPC, emphasis added)." Having the Holy Spirit and His fruit within while attempting to handle situations of carnality will allow a person to recognize where the problem is and make needed adjustments.

We must mature in the capacity to allow the spiritual nature to dominate and override the carnal nature. If our identity is carnal, we will continually have mental health issues, and it opens the door to mental health diagnosis. The problem is NOT mental health issues; it is the carnal nature (that has not been crucified, or dealt with) that gives way to the mental health issues, which produces the works of the flesh. A person matures in recognizing the role of the Holy Spirit, and the full Community of God. As this maturity occurs, the person can allow Holy Spirit to dwell within and produce the fruit of the Spirit, and cauterize the works of the flesh; which are the works of carnality that opens the door to sin that is crouching at the door (as in Genesis 4:7). This all occurs because the carnal mind was allowed to remain uncontested. We cannot neglect maturing in understanding who God is, and who we are in Him – which is a summarized definition of the components of righteousness. As a person matures in this understanding, carnality is crucified, and fruit are produced; and the person is made whole as in 1 Thessalonians 5:23.

If we do not mature in the things of God, the carnal mind will lead, as in the Romans 7 battle. The evil that is always with me is the carnal nature. We must crucify those manifestations, not the behaviors, but the manifestations. These expose the degree to which there is a lack of identity. It is like navigating, if the coordinates are off a few degrees, you will not arrive to the desired destination. I have coined the phrase "carnality-ometer," which identifies areas of carnality in one's life, and cannot be mis-calibrated. Therefore, we must mature and recognize where we are on the scale of carnality which is evidenced by the list identifying the carnal manifestation of the flesh discussed earlier.

When we crucify the carnal mind, we are then able to live *My Body, His Life* as discussed in Dr. Paul G. Trulin's book. The theme scripture for his book is: "Truly, truly I say to you, unless a grain of wheat falls into the earth and dies, it remains alone; but if it dies, it bears much fruit (John 12:24 NASB)." Trulin's book is helpful in identifying how to crucify, put to death, or die to the carnal nature and live an empowered life for Christ.

"It is evident that a person belongs to the flesh if he comports himself like an ordinary man and sins often. No matter how much spiritual teaching he knows or how many spiritual experiences he purports to have had or how much effective service he has rendered: none of these makes him less carnal if he remains undelivered from his peculiar temperament, his temper, his selfishness, his contention, his vainglory, his unforgiving or unloving spirit."[103] This sounds like strongholds. Know that "with this imagery in mind that the inspired writers of the Bible adapted the word *stronghold* to define powerful, vigorously protected spiritual realities."[104]

Through previous in-depth study etched in my memory, I found that a stronghold is a house made of mental thoughts at a young age for future occupation, of either godly or evil forces. Therefore, as a child, if a person is constantly built up and given thoughts that they are

---

[103] Watchman Nee. *The Spiritual Man*. (New York: Christian Fellowship Publishers Inc, 1977). 88-89.
[104] Francis Frangipane. *The Three Battlegrounds: An In-Depth View of the Three Arenas of Spiritual Warfare: the Mind, the Church and the Heavenly Places*, 2nd ed. (Cedar Rapids: Arrow Publications, 2010). 28.

a mighty man of God, as they grow up and life happens, the house or thought life of "I am a mighty man of God" will rise up. Examples of demonic strongholds that must be pulled down are thoughts like "You will never be anything — nobody wants to hear from you, a woman, single, not raised in the church, with no credentials behind your name" — all of these were strongholds that the enemy spoke to me from the day I got saved and fought with my call. I was fighting because those childish strongholds were holding me.

Paul discusses the pulling down of these strongholds here: "For although we live in the natural realm, we don't wage a military campaign employing human weapons, using manipulation to achieve our aims. Instead, our spiritual weapons are energized with divine power to effectively dismantle the defenses behind which people hide. We can demolish every deceptive fantasy that opposes God and break through every arrogant attitude that is raised up in defiance of the true knowledge of God. We capture, like prisoners of war, every thought and insist that it bow in obedience to the Anointed One (2 Corinthians 10:3-5 TPT)."

Another stronghold is that of mistakes, shame, and guilt (M.S.G.); which can cause people to want to escape or just end their life. Suicide is more prevalent (stronger) because the enemy has been building strongholds (houses of mental thoughts at a young age for future occupation). He has been building these fortified houses for years, (his house is a house of imprisonment to keep you in, and not allow anyone else to come in). No one knows about these silent strongholds, which is why people seem to fall through the trap door in the bottom. But the house (the stronghold) must be demolished by the power and the presence of God, and by understanding your identity as being created in the image of the Community of God, and the fact that you have dominion over the enemy. The battle, or strain, occurs when a person tries to make sense of life's happenings in the natural, by looking for the image and the identity in their family and their life circumstances.

Isaiah 26:3 is where the carnal mind battle is fought, the battleground of the mind. The kingdom of heaven suffers violence, and the violent taketh by force. You will forcefully keep your mind on God, not on the manifestations of things that could cause you to not be in peace, not on previous mistakes, shame or guilt (M.S.G.); nor looking to one's family for clarity.

"The entire universe is standing on tiptoe, yearning to see the unveiling of God's glorious sons and daughters (Romans 8:9 TPT)!" The reason the earth is yearning, groaning and moaning as in some versions, for the sons of God to be manifested is because the sons of God must mature and be manifested through the carnal nature (and all that is in the world). Therefore, the world is waiting. These sons of God are maturing out of carnality to gain the ability to operate in the heavenly realm. It is about dominion. You can only operate in dominion to the degree that you understand identity – the Imago Dei – the creation mandate.

The Screwtape Element is to convince huMANkind to remain carnal, never maturing, only identifying with the carnal nature and never fully realizing that it is *My Body, His Life*. Once again, the battle is about worship. Carnal worship is unacceptable. "Worship cannot be isolated or relegated to just one place, time, or segment of our lives. We cannot verbally thank and praise God while living lives of selfishness and carnality."[105]

---

[105] John F. MacArthur *Worship: The Ultimate Priority*. (Chicago: Moody Publishers, 2012). 43.

Distorted Identity – Through Fear, Rejection, ACEs, Trauma, and Rebellion

Mental health issues and the immature carnal nature can create identity crises. As well as distorted identity that is produced through fear, rejection, Adverse Childhood Experiences ACEs, trauma and rebellion. In *Scared Sick*, 'fear' is defined "as our most fundamental emotional and physical response to a perceived threat, triggering the chain of physical responses commonly known as *fight-or-flight*."[106]

The book titled *When Someone You Love is Someone You Hate* describes the powerful role of fear in the distortion of identity. "The two fears, fear of abandonment and fear of being smothered, are integral parts of the love-hate relationship… The person who fears being abandoned is likely to smother whatever is closest. And the person being smothered is likely to fear that others will attempt this smothering process. He or she will become overpowering in the relationship in an attempt to exert control and prevent smothering… Thus the mantle of unhealthy fear is passed on from one generation to the other. Fear is bred throughout the family and passed on to the next unhealthy generation.

"The normal is replaced with the abnormal and reproduced with the development of each new relationship … Love-hate relationships originate from an identifiable source, then progress along a predictable path, and are resolved with a proven prescription… At the base of this confusing dichotomy of feeling there are three negative emotions that combine to foster the development of the love-hate bind. These three emotions of great negative impact are fear, anger, and guilt."[107]

---

[106] Robin Karr-Morse, and Meredith S. Wiley. *Scared Sick: The Role of Childhood Trauma in Adult Disease.* (New York, Basic Books, 2012). 18.
[107] Stephen Arterburn, and David A. Stoop. *When Someone You Love is Someone You Hate.* (W Publishing Group, 1988). 34, 23.

These three key emotions present a destructive cycle in that the unresolved *fear* of childhood produces a "helpless belief that the world will never be a safe and wonderful place for me to live." Next, the helplessness felt from the continued fear manifests in anger, "because I feel inadequate to remake the past." Finally, the lack of the ability to "remake the past" produces within me a feeling of guilt because I refuse to forgive myself and others.[108]

Feelings can distort identity. "Ephemeral sensations we call 'feelings' – our emotions – fuel the stress response. In fact, our feelings, often disguised, repressed or denied, are in constant chemical communication with our brains – and consequently with the all key systems in our bodies – about the status of our health and safety."[109] These distorted feelings and emotions are a recipe for distorted identity.

Another element that empowers fear is pride. These two elements are highlighted in the book *Rejection - Its Fruits and Its Roots: A Scriptural Understanding of Rejection, How it Works and How to Minister*. "Both fear and pride are present in differing degrees when responding in the flesh to rejection… The pride reaction to rejection is to respond in rebellion, stubbornness, scorning, bitterness, accusation and paranoia… Stubbornness and scorning (or scoffing) are also related to each other and generally accompany rebellion and bitterness.[110]

Arthur Null further offers the following descriptions:
- "Rebellion brings divination (witchcraft), religious spirits, shame, humiliation, confusion, bondage, idolatry and whoredom.

---

[108] Stephen Arterburn, and David A. Stoop. *When Someone You Love is Someone You Hate*. (W Publishing Group, 1988). 47.
[109] Robin Karr-Morse, and Meredith S. Wiley. *Scared Sick: The Role of Childhood Trauma in Adult Disease*. (New York, Basic Books, 2012). 19.
[110] William G. Null. *Rejection - Its Fruits and Its Roots: A Scriptural Understanding of Rejection, How it Works and How to Minister*. (Impact Christian Books Inc, Kirkwood, MO, 2005). 251-252.

- Stubbornness brings deception, unteachableness, stubborn self-will, selfishness, witchcraft (control of others) and whoredom.

- Bitterness will bring a bitter root, infirmity spirits (with pain and disability), unforgiveness, idolatry/whoredom, and bondage."[111]

Often times, these issues resulting from rejection are labeled as a family curse. Arthur Null additionally states that: "Generational curses cause us to repeat the sins of the fathers. The curse of whoredom (Hosea 4:6-14) causes many problems, including adultery and fornication, which result in rejection. Since the outward reaction to rejection is pride, rebellion, and stubbornness, these behaviors cause more rejection. The pattern is reinforced and continues in a never-ending spiral downward, unless interrupted by the healing power of God's might, love, and prayers of deliverance."[112]

Distorted identity usually manifests as a result of adverse childhood experiences ACEs. "The ACE Study is ongoing collaborative research between the Centers for Disease Control and Prevention in Atlanta, GA, and Kaiser Permanente in San Diego, CA… The study reveals staggering proof of the health, social, and economic risks that result from childhood trauma."[113] However, the disheartening fact is that the ACE study "is basically a post-fact scorecard of the broken hearts and lives of children raised in a traumatic environment."[114] The

---

[111] William G. Null. *Rejection - Its Fruits and Its Roots: A Scriptural Understanding of Rejection, How it Works and How to Minister.* (Impact Christian Books Inc, Kirkwood, MO, 2005). 252.
[112] Ibid. 17.
[113] John R. Trayser. *The Aces Revolution!: The Impact of Adverse Childhood Experiences.* (Scotts Valley: Createspace Independent Publishing Platform, 2016). 1.

[114] Ibid. 1.

Screwtape Element is to accouter believers with the armor of distorted identity at a young age, which is an entry way for mental health issues in adulthood.

Similarly, another Screwtape Element is of the role of trauma in the believer's life. A working definition of trauma is any experience which by its nature is in excess of what we can manage or bear. "Trauma – especially for children who have not yet learned language – tends to be stored in the brain not primarily as a conscious, rational, language-based experience in *declarative memory* but rather as a somatic or 'feeling' memory stored in unconscious or *procedural memory*. Somatic memories may surface later in life in the form of physical symptoms that seem to have no discernable cause, such as a chronic pain, headache, or fibromyalgia."[115] This brain connection with trauma and mental health issues will be discussed more extensively in the next section.

The following excerpt addresses the history and role of epigenetics and mental health disparities:

> Developmental biologist Conrad Waddington first coined the term *epigenetics* in the 1940s; *epi-* means 'above,' so *epigenome* is meant to convey 'above the genome.' Epigenetics is the newly emerging branch of biology that deals with the effects of external influences on gene expression. At the biological level, this is where nature and nurture become indistinguishable. The *genome* contains DNA, the blueprints or codes for making the proteins that are the building blocks of life. But DNA is not all that the genome carries. Even more of the genome is made up of non-coding regions that circulate around DNA and regulate how DNA functions, causing certain genes to be expressed while others are repressed. So, along with DNA that remains stable, we inherit dynamic chemical processes within our cells that surround and communicate instructions to our genes, telling them when to be active and when not to be, essentially activating or silencing their expression.
>
> The influences on our DNA include both developmental and environmental factors ... *The Epigenetics of Mental Health*. Research on the epigenetics of emotional disease is so new that hypotheses and findings are announced weekly. Since the completion of

---

[115] Robin Karr-Morse, and Meredith S. Wiley. *Scared Sick: The Role of Childhood Trauma in Adult Disease.* (New York, Basic Books, 2012). 26.

the mapping of the human genome and the subsequent recognition that the findings did little to explain many forms of illness, virtually every major form of mental illness is being scrutinized for epigenetic underpinnings… Some scientists believe that depression – which is characterized by inertia and a total inability to focus – is a physical illness typified by a reduction in the size of the hippocampus. There is a growing belief, in fact, that most so-called mental illnesses are nothing less than physical illnesses of the brain that in turn have led to psychological dysfunction.[116]

Another factor to take into account regarding distorted identity from childhood events is that of a slumbering spirit. John and Paula Sanford have ministered to many people with a slumbering personal spirit. The following excerpt describes a portion of the healing journey to identify the state of the spirit: "It may be necessary to explain how his spirit can hold resentment and judgments toward his parents when he is unaware of it. We help him to identify the fruits in his life, which necessarily have roots. We assure him that just as he received salvation by faith, not by feeling, so he need not try to feel again what his spirit actually felt towards his parents; he needs only by faith to acknowledge that, because the fruit is evident, sins of resentment may be there and receive forgiveness by faith."[117]

Furthermore, persons with "slumbering spirits also need to be reassured that God has His own timetable and that in His eyes, they are not behind schedule. One reason they fell asleep in the first place is because, as children, there was no comfort. They had to learn to rely on themselves. Therefore, if God awakes their spirits too soon, they might rely too much on their own ability to hear God, to sense, and to feel. They need to be told that God will indeed restore the functions of their spirits – but only after their hearts have learned to trust in the

---

[116] Robin Karr-Morse, and Meredith S. Wiley. *Scared Sick: The Role of Childhood Trauma in Adult Disease*. (New York, Basic Books, 2012). 152 and 176.

[117] Sandford, John L., and Paula Sandford. *Healing the Wounded Spirit*. Victory House Publishers, 1985. 52.

hearts of others."[118] The slumbering spirit is definitely a cause of distorted identity, and awakening the spirit is the needed anecdote as in Ephesians 5:14.

The Brain

As mentioned in the section on the body in chapter two, there is a difference between the mind and the brain. The empowered identity is evidenced through the acquired understanding of the scientific working of the brain. I found several references to the fact that our brains are flexible and have the capacity to control our reactions to life's situations because "God has designed our brain to work for us and not to control us."[119] With that being said, believers need to know that "we are not victims of our biology or circumstances. How we react to the events and circumstances of life can have an enormous impact on our mental and even physical health."[120]

Spirit controlled temperament is the goal and brings much assistance with managing the thought life. "Thoughts are real, physical things that occupy mental real estate. Moment by moment, every day, you are changing the structure of your brain through your thinking. When we hope, it is an activity of the mind that changes the structure of our brain in a positive and normal direction."[121] That is so important because only the mind can take away what it creates, which is further described as neuroplasticity. Dr. Caroline Leaf shares that neuroplasticity is God's design for renewing the mind. Actually, humans "are designed to

---

[118] Sandford, John L., and Paula Sandford. *Healing the Wounded Spirit*. Victory House Publishers, 1985. 55.

[119] Caroline Leaf. *Switch On Your Brain: The Key to Peak Happiness, Thinking, and Health*. (Ada: Baker Books, 2013). 82.

[120] Ibid, 20.
[121] Ibid. 19.

stand outside yourself and observe your own thinking *and change it* (Romans 12:2; 2 Corinthians 15:5; Philippians 3:13-14)."[122]

Quantum physics aligns with scripture and is another way of admiring God. "When we operate in our normal love design – which is being made in God's image (Genesis 1:27) – we are able to change the shape of our DNA for the better"[123] This is a perfect summarization of the Imago Dei. "Our DNA is designed to react to the language of our thoughts and resultant words as well as the biological signals… Our *Perfect You* activates our DNA and structural change occurs in the brain: this is intelligence and wisdom."[124]

Caroline Leaf further summarizes that: "You have been designed for deep, intellectual thought (Psalm 139:14). **You are wired for love**, and fear is a learned and not a natural response (2 Timothy 1:7)."[125] Many of us were once tormented by fear; when in reality we were wired for love. Yet we learned fear through the distorted identity.

Being wired for love empowers believers to regularly walk in the power, love, and sound mind of 2 Timothy 1:7, instead of walking in fear. It also empowers huMANkind to make better choices in general. "Choices are real, you are free to make choices about how you focus your attention, and this affects how the chemicals, proteins, and wiring of your brain change and function."[126] Choose love. Choose life.

Free will is involved in the choices we make. "Behold, I have found only this, that God made people upright, but they have sought out many schemes (Ecclesiastes 7:29 NASB)." To better understand the significance of free will, Dr. Leaf offers that the "standard

---

[122] Ibid, 25.
[123] Ibid, 36.
[124] Leaf, 60.
[125] Ibid, 26, emphasis added.
[126] Ibid, 38.

definition of free will is a set of capacities for imagining future courses of action, deliberating about one's reason for choosing them, planning one's actions in the face of competing desires."[127] Free will is also impacted by the health of one's brain, and other contributing neuro factors. The following list of insights about the free will and the genome factor will illustrate this connection. In summary, these points reveal the empowerment of realizing that brain health is an important factor in regards to personality, fulfilling destiny, and making choices.

- "We are born with our genome, but we can protect our epigenome. We used to think that our genetic code was laid down from the beginning of life and that whatever we got was a life sentence. But the new understanding of the epigenetic code brings great optimism to this often bleak prognosis. Epigenetic patterns can change through life, and little changes can create huge differences."[128]

- "The Geodesic Information Processing Theory deals with the science of thought. It is a description of how we think, choose, and build thoughts and the impact of this on our brain and behavior."[129]

- "Collectively, these studies show us that the good, the bad, and the ugly do come down through the generations. But your mind is the signal – the epigenetic factor – that switches these genes on or off. Therefore, you are not

---

[127] Ibid, 43.
[128] Robin Karr-Morse, and Meredith S. Wiley. *Scared Sick: The Role of Childhood Trauma in Adult Disease.* (New York, Basic Books, 2012). 166.
[129] Caroline Leaf. *Switch On Your Brain: The Key to Peak Happiness, Thinking, and Health.* (Ada: Baker Books, 2013). 134.

destined to live out the negative patterns of your forbearers, but you can instead make a life choice to overcome them by tweaking their expression."[130]

- "The sins of the parents create a *predisposition*, not a *destiny*. You are not responsible for something you are predisposed to because of ancestral decision. You are responsible, however, to be aware of the predispositions, evaluate them, and choose to eliminate them."[131]

- Dr. Daniel Amen said that "as I began to look at my patients' brains, one simple question occurred to me again and again: what is the organ of personality? It's our brain. If someone has a difficult personality, their brain may be the cause, and there is a chance it could be improved, leaving them with a happier and healthier life."[132]

Aftermath: Critical Spirit, Codependency, Anxiety – Depression, ADD, and Addictions

A critical spirit is formed as a symptom, or result of the distorted identity discussed earlier. "Why are some people so judgmental? A critical spirit doesn't appear out of nowhere – it is created and nurtured by past negative experiences. Don't just focus on the present problem. Instead, look back to the past. What could have produced the critical spirit and what continues to perpetuate it? Scripture points to the source of contentious behavior in: What causes fights and quarrels among you? Don't they come from your desires that battle within

---

[130] Ibid, 69.
[131] Ibid, 59-60.
[132] Amen, Daniel G. *Change Your Brain, Change Your Life: The Breakthrough Program for Conquering Anxiety, Depression, Obsessiveness, Anger, and Impulsiveness.* (New York: Harmony, 2015). 334.

you?"[133] These next two bullets expose the concepts of the critical spirit adapted from an unstable childhood, or ACEs:

- "The most common cause of a critical spirit is living in a home where criticism abounds – where parents model a critical spirit before their children. Growing up in such a home where critical comments are continually hurled can cause a child to be overly critical in adulthood. After all, with children, more is *caught* than *taught*."[134]
- "Many children who were assaulted with wounding words resort to criticism as a means of self-defense. To try to lessen the impact of their own emotional pain, *they stay on the attack*."[135] Or as I have found, hurting people hurt people. The cycle must be broken and healed.

False burdens, feelings of heaviness and oppression can come upon a person through the constant bombardments from a person with a critical spirit; thus, causing the person to be codependent to the person with the critical spirit. A person with a high capacity to be codependent, will cause (or draw) critically spirited people to be able to operate in stealth. Note: people that are raised by broken people, inadvertently pass on the brokenness to the next generation, unawares. Even if the child was never abused, the brokenness can still be passed on to the next generation through the ACEs.

---

[133] Hunt, June. Critical Spirit: Confronting the Heart of a Critic, 7th ed. Peabody, MA: Hendrickson Publishers, 2017. 32.

[134] Ibid, 33.

[135] Ibid, 35.

- "Codependency became the word that describes the dysfunctional behavior of family members seeking to adapt to the destructive behavior of the alcoholic. Codependency is a relationship addiction. Just as the alcoholic is dependent on alcohol, the codependent is dependent on *being needed* by the alcoholic, or on being needed by someone who is dependent."[136]

- "Codependency can be compared to the sin of depending on false gods that are powerless to help or depending on a broken water well that won't hold water. It simply won't work."[137]

The plan of God is for children to be raised with a knowledge of Him, so that when they grow older they will be dependent on God, not on their parents, or another person; which can create an expectation for people to provide what only God can. For myself personally, having grown up experiencing dysfunction, I am not accusing our parents/guardians of anything. I am simply noting that identity is found in *Him*, not *them*. I lived an active account of Isaiah 26:3, to keep my focus on Him to remain in perfect peace, and no longer focus on my parents and previous home life situations.

Codependence may be caused by unresolved childhood pain, and by being reared by immature grownups who operate out of carnality. The writer of the book of Hebrews addressed the carnality of needing milk only, instead of solid food: "Milk is for beginners,

---

[136] June Hunt. *Codependency: Balancing an Unbalanced Relationship*. (Rose Publishing, 2013). 15.
[137] Ibid. 16.

inexperienced in God's ways; **<u>solid food is for the mature, who have some practice in telling right from wrong</u>** (Hebrews 5:13 MSG, emphasis added)."

Codependent people often times shift from one addiction to another. This is referred to as a replacement theory or the manifestation of secondary addictions. Often not viewed as an addiction, perfectionism and workaholic-ism may be evident. Some people work to escape painful situations, or perform to gain approval. Others perform to survive and to be validated. The establishment of godly boundaries is required. Boundaries in relationships that will always direct people to the Person of God, not of self. Sometimes, when someone is healed from a distorted identity, those who are attached to them and benefiting from this, may not be able to change with them. This creates relationship strains in the opposite direction.

The following three pages are tables adapted from Dr. Daniel Amen's book *Change Your Brain, Change Your Life* which depict a summary of mental health issues the Amen Clinics have encountered over the course of their existence. These same areas may manifest in people due to the identity crisis concerns we have discussed thus far. I have intentionally omitted his suggestions for medication as a part of the treatment plan, because I am not qualified to address that aspect. However, the quoted information will prove beneficial to those getting acquainted with the symptoms, brain findings, suggested supplements, dietary and other intervention actions.

Summary Chart of the Amen Clinics 7 Types of Anxiety and Depression (Amen, page 284-285)

TYPE	SYMPTOMS	BRAIN FINDINGS/NEURO-TRANSMITTER ISSUE	SUPPLEMENTS	DIET AND OTHER INTERVENTIONS
1. Pure Anxiety	Anxious, tense, nervous, predicts the worst, self-medicates to calm	High basal ganglia/low GABA levels	GABA, B6, magnesium, DHA fish oil	Meditation, hypnosis
2. Pure Depression	Depression, feeling hopeless, low energy, poor appetite, insomnia	Low PFC plus high limbic activity/low dopamine (DA)	SAMe, EPA fish oil	Exercise
3. Mixed Anxiety and Depression	Combination of symptoms from Types 1 and 2	High basal ganglia and limbic actitivy/low GABA and DA	GABA, B6, magnesium, SAMe, EPA/DHA fish oil	meditation, hypnosis, and exercise
4. Overfocused Anxiety and Depression	Overfocused, worrying, oppositional, holds grudges	Increased ACG/low serotonin (S)	5-HTP, saffron, or St. John's wort	Higher carb, lower protein diet, exercise
5. Temporal Lobe Anxiety and Depression	Temper problems, mood instability, irritablity, memory problems, learning disabilities	Abnormal TLs/low GABA	GABA, B6, magnesium for calming, or huperzine A, accetyl-l-carnitine, vinpocetine, gingko for memory	Higher protein, lower carb diet, exercise
6. Cyclic Anxiety and Depression	Mood cycles (Bipolar, cyclothymia, severe PMS)	High focal limbic activity / low GABA	GABA, B6, magnesium	Higher protein, lower carb diet
7. Unfocused Anxiety and Depression	Sadness, anxiety, low energy, cognitive problems	Overall low activity, brain may look toxic	Green tea, rhodiola, or L-tyrosine	Medical workup of potential causes of toxicity

138

---

[138] Amen, Daniel G. *Change Your Brain, Change Your Life: The Breakthrough Program for Conquering Anxiety, Depression, Obsessiveness, Anger, and Impulsiveness*. (New York: Harmony, 2015). 284-285.

Summary Chart of the Amen Clinics 7 Types of ADD (Amen, page 276-277)

TYPE	SYMPTOMS	BRAIN FINDINGS/NEURO-TRANSMITTER ISSUE	SUPPLEMENTS	DIET AND OTHER INTERVENTIONS
1. Classic ADD	Inattentive, distracted, disorganized, impulsive, hyperactive	Low PFC, and cerebellum, low dopamine (DA)	Green tea, rhodiola, or L-tyrosine plus EPA fish oil	Higher protein, lower carb diet, exercise
2. Inattentive ADD	Inattentive, distracted, disorganized, *not* very impulsive, hyperactive	Low PFC, and cerebellum, low (DA)	Green tea, rhodiola, or L-tyrosine plus EPA fish oil	Higher protein, lower carb diet, exercise
3. Overfocused ADD	Inattentive plus overfocused, worrying, oppositional, holds grudges	Low PFC and increased ACG, low serotonin (S)	Green tea, rhodiola, or L-tyrosine plus EPA fish oil	Higher carb, lower protein diet, exercise
4. Temporal Lobe ADD	Temper problems, mood instability, irritability, memory problems, learing disabilities	Abnormal TLs/Low GABA	GABA, B6, magnesium for calming, or huperzine A, acetyl-l-carnitine, vinpocetine, ginkgo for memory PLUS EPA fish oil	Higher protein, lower carb diet
5. Limbic ADD	Innattentive plus chronic low-level sadness	Low PFC plus high limbic activity	SAMe plus EPA fish oil	Higher protein, lower carb diet, exercise
6. Ring of Fire ADD	Inattentive plus hyperactive, impulsive, mood instability, sensitve to noise and touch	Excessive brain activity/Low DA and GABA levels	GABA, 5-HTP, and L-tyrosine PLUS EPA/DHA fish oil	Balanced diet between protein and carbs
7. Anxious ADD	Innattentive plus anxious, tense, nervous, predicts the worst, self-medicates to calm	Low PFC and high basal ganglia/low DA and GABA levels	Green tea, rhodiola, or L-tyrosine plus GABA, B6, magnesium plus EPA/DHA fish oil	Balanced diet between protein and carbs, meditation and hypnosis

---

[139] Amen, Daniel G. *Change Your Brain, Change Your Life: The Breakthrough Program for Conquering Anxiety, Depression, Obsessiveness, Anger, and Impulsiveness*. (New York: Harmony, 2015). 276-277.

Summary Chart of the Amen Clinics 6 Types of Addicts (Amen, page 292)

TYPE	SYMPTOMS	BRAIN FINDINGS/NEURO-TRANSMITTER ISSUE	SUPPLEMENTS
1. Compulsive Addicts	Overfocused, worrying, trouble letting go of hurts	Increased ACG/low serotonin (S)	5-HTP, inositol, saffron, or St. John's wort
2. Impulsive Addicts	Inattentive, impulsive, easily distracted	Low PFC/low dopamine (DA)	Green tea, rhodiola, or L-tyrosine
3. Impulsive-Compulsive Addicts	Combination of types 1 and 2	High ACG plus low PFC/low S and DA	5-HTP plus green tea and rhodiola
4. Sad or Emotional Addicts	Sad or depressed mood, winter blues, carbohydrate cravings, loss of interest, sleeps a lot, low energy, self-medicates to improve mood	High limbic activity, low PFC/check vitamin D and DHEA levels	SAMe, vitamin D, or DHEA if needed
5. Anxious Addicts	Anxious, tense, nervous, predicts the worst, self-medicates to calm	High basal ganglia/low GABA levels	GABA, B6, magnesium
6. Temporal Lobe Addicts	Temper problems, mood instability, memory problems, learning disabilities	Abnormal TL	GABA, B6, magnesium for calming, or huperzine A, acetyl-l-carnitine, vinpocetine, gingo for memory

140

---

[140] Amen, Daniel G. *Change Your Brain, Change Your Life: The Breakthrough Program for Conquering Anxiety, Depression, Obsessiveness, Anger, and Impulsiveness.* (New York: Harmony, 2015). 292.

CHAPTER FIVE: Empowered Identity

The empowered identity is that of being an overcomer of the faulty identities that have been received prior to fully understanding the Community of God, the composition of the tri-part huMANkind, and the warfare for worship by the forces of darkness contending for the light within mankind. This empowerment is achieved by recognizing the true battle for the thought life, which is where identity crises develops, forming distortions to identity and manifested mental health issues. The Holy Spirit plays an intricate role in empowering identity by assisting believers to know the Community of God personally, and relationally. Additionally, the Holy Spirit contends to be a key role in the forgiveness process, inner healing, and understanding personality development. Lastly, reiterating the understanding of scientific aspects of the brain will enable believers to achieve somatically holistic healing and learn how to show up authentically in his or her Imago Dei; in their true identity.

Salvation and Deliverance

Recognition of the need to understand identity and the evident identity crisis should make people ask, like the Roman jailer "after he brought them out, he said, 'Sirs, what must I do to be saved?' (Acts 16:30 NASB)." The Greek word for saved is *sozo* and it means "to be healed or made whole; to keep safe and sound; or to rescue from danger, destruction or perishing."[141] Distorted identity will definitely create this state within a person's thinking.

---

[141] Bible Search and Study Tools – Blue Letter Bible. (Accessed April 4, 2021). https://www.blueletterbible.org/.

"Each of us needs Jesus as Lord and Savior, not so that we can acquire an Imago Dei, but because we must surrender our lives to Him in order to uncover it … Know that it is not only Jesus' physical body that is buried, but the fallen nature of man with it. Everything old passes away as the Son of God descends to the very depths of our separation from God, and sets us free."[142]

Salvation is a one-time event of acknowledging the plan of redemption. "Salvation was God's Plan A, and not Plan B."[143] However, there will be many deliverances in the life of each person. The psalmist puts it this way: "Blessed be the Lord, Who bears our burdens and carries us day by day, even the God Who is our salvation! Selah [pause, and calmly think of that]! God is to us a **God of deliveranceS and salvation**; and to God the Lord belongs escape from death [setting us free] (Psalm 68:19-20 AMPC, emphasis added)."

I described these two verses like this in the book *Christians On Assignment – Talking About Obedience*: "We can see that we are saved, salvation is ours, yet we rely on God to help us through deliverance after deliverance from habits that we find in ourselves... Notice salvation is singular, it only takes one time, and deliverance is plural, causing us to see that the deliverance *portion* may take place over and over again. Also, in the King James Version of Psalm 68:19 it reads *Blessed be the Lord, who daily loadeth us with **benefits**, even the God of our salvation.* Benefits is plural – these deliverances and benefits can come daily. Thank You Lord! We grow from faith to faith, and glory to glory."[144]

---

[142] Catherine Skurja. *Paradox Lost: Uncovering the True Identity in Christ*. (Imago Dei Resources LLC, 2012). 44 and 188.
[143] Richard Rohr and Mike Morrell. *The Divine Dance: The Trinity and Your Transformation*. (Whitaker House, 2016. Kindle edition), 28.
[144] Paulette Denise. *Christians On Assignment Talking About Obedience*. (Houston: A Portion, 2010). 30.

Repentance is a required element in deliverance; a complete change of mind. *Metanoia* is the Greek word used to describe the type of repentance required for the entrance into the kingdom of God discussed in Mark 1:15. The deeper meaning of this word "means not so much being sorry …but is understood as a 'turnabout.' *Metanoia* includes turning away from our identification with our outer mask and confronting what lies behind that mask, what looks like an inner adversary or enemy."[145] Masks can be cloaked as service unto the Lord, or people pleasing, which are other ways the Screwtape Element is subtly advanced.

"Many Christians are trying their best to walk as children of light, but they too often fall into what we call 'PO' – *performance orientation* – striving, disillusionment, and ultimately, self-condemnation. They are blindsided and driven from deep within by that of which they have been unaware. They have rightly celebrated salvation as a free gift (Ephesians 2:4-5, 8; Romans 6:23), but they may not have understood that they are to grow up (1 Peter 2:2; Ephesians 3:14-19) or that they are to work out that salvation in fear and trembling (Philippians 2:12)…They 'press on' in terms of managing their behavior rather than renewing their minds (Romans 12:2) and receiving a new heart and spirit (Psalm 51; Ezekiel 36:26), which would naturally result in changed behavior."[146]

Deliverance in the soulish areas of identity is essential to the continued walk of the empowered identity. Worship is an integral part of identity. Worship is a posture of the heart, therefore, the heart must be cultivated through deliverance of wrong beliefs to truly engage in worship. "The channel through which the Lord extends Himself, even into our past, is our love and worship of Him… Therefore, it is essential to both the salvation of our souls and our

---

[145] Sanford, John A. The Kingdom Within: The Inner Meaning of Jesus' Sayings. HarperOne, 1987. 82.
[146] Sandford, John L., and Paula Sandford. *Healing the Wounded Spirit*. Victory House Publishers, 1985. 1-2.

protection in warfare that we be worshipers. The ship which safely carries us through the storms of adversity is worship."[147]

Believers must be free to worship. Free, unhindered by the cares of this world and the wiles of the adversary. In a sense, believers must be liberated. "The deliverance of the soul is different than the liberation of …the spirit. The soul is made of life's events: the memories and hopes, loves and hates, experiences and reactions. It is your personality, intellect and emotions. Your spirit, however, is the silent observer when you dream; it is the evaluator of your thoughts… We must identify in the spirit the subtle shift that moves from trusting God to anxiously manipulating other people."[148]

Francis Frangipane addresses the integration and liberation of believers the following way: "Christianity is the most psychological of all religions because of this emphasis that it places on the inner development of the individual and the important role that it assigns to the ego as the bearer of consciousness… Becoming a complete person is a matter of psychological development, but not of psychologizing. Totality comes when life is lived completely, when the demands of both inner and outer realities are met consciously."[149]

As stated earlier, spiritual maturity is a key element to balancing the dichotomy of identity and mental health issues. Spiritual maturity is referring to recognizing the Imago Dei of the spirit, and maturing the huMANkind elements of the spirit through the renewal of the mind, which is the soul. Therefore, an environment for maturity must be cultivated. "When the right kind of environment is created, deadness will disappear and spiritual bread and life

---

[147] Francis Frangipane. *The Three Battlegrounds: An In-Depth View of the Three Arenas of Spiritual Warfare: the Mind, the Church and the Heavenly Places*, 2nd ed. (Cedar Rapids: Arrow Publications, 2010). 92.
[148] Ibid. 153.
[149] Sanford, John A. The Kingdom Within: The Inner Meaning of Jesus' Sayings. HarperOne, 1987. 173.

will flow. People will drink of the water of life fully. When spiritual hunger is met, they leave God's house with a satisfaction that brings rest to their spirit and encouragement for the tasks and burdens of life ahead of them."[150]

The Screwtape Element is to generate an environment of chaos and carnality. However, the anecdote is the help of the Holy Spirit as referenced in Revelation 22:17 and Isaiah 55:1 which describe a thirst by which the soul is supported, strengthened, renewed, and refreshed. It is the thirsty soul that shall be quenched with the rivers of living water from a well that won't run dry, by being centered in identity as Imago Dei.

The Role of Holy Spirit

The Holy Spirit can be grieved as described in Ephesians 4:29-32. He can also be quenched as in 1 Thessalonians 5:19. Therefore, the Screwtape Element is to cause believers to grieve or quench the Holy Spirit through distorted identity and manifested mental health issues. This is an important role of the counselor in counseling to assist in removing these hindrances and emancipate believers to walk in their empowered identity.

Believers can position themselves to allow the Holy Spirit to deposit truth and direction in their spirit as they grow in trusting God. The following list of scriptures highlight the important role of the Person of the Holy Spirit in the lives of believers:

- But the Comforter (Counselor, Helper, Intercessor, Advocate, Strengthener, Standby), the Holy Spirit, Whom the Father will send in My name [in My place, to represent Me and act on My behalf], He will teach you all things. And He will

---

[150] Paul G. Trulin. *My Body, His Life*, 11th ed. (Sacramento: Paul Trulin Ministries, 1989). 101.

cause you to recall (will remind you of, bring to your remembrance) everything I have told you. (John 14:26 AMPC).

- Lean on, trust in, and be confident in the Lord with all your heart and mind and do not rely on your own insight or understanding. In all your ways know, recognize, and acknowledge Him, and He will direct and make straight and plain your paths. (Proverbs 3:5-6 AMPC).

- But as for you, the anointing (the sacred appointment, the unction) which you received from Him abides [permanently] in you; [so] then you have no need that anyone should instruct you. But just as His anointing teaches you concerning everything and is true and is no falsehood, so you must abide in (live in, never depart from) Him [being rooted in Him, knit to Him], just as [His anointing] has taught you [to do] 1 John 2:27 AMPC).

A key role of the Holy Spirit is to assist believers in the Renewal of the Mind process. He is the Spirit of Truth who is also responsible to teach us how to behave and riposte in various situations according to Galatians 5:22-23 and John 16:13. "The Holy Spirit will guide us, if we *choose* to listen to Him, and show us the correct way to 'consciously veto' our thinking, feeling, and choosing."[151] In short, He empowers our thinking. "Many Christians have tried to forget the sins of the past by ignoring them rather than by allowing the Holy

---

[151] Leaf, Caroline. The Perfect You: A Blueprint for Identity. Ada: Baker Books, 2017. 93.

Spirit to search the innermost parts of their heart, see Psalm 139:23-24."[152] This is a profound example of the role of the Holy Spirit!

"God created us for relationship with Him. Nothing else will satisfy this need to pray continuously and set up a constant internal dialogue with the Holy Spirit, so that we stay addicted to Him, offering up our minds and bodies as a living sacrifice every day (Romans 12:2)… God has given us the ability to break free from any toxic pattern, and this happens when we are in the *Perfect You* (Romans 8:37-39)."[153] Hence, Dr. Caroline Leaf was describing how another role of Holy Spirit is to *help with* the removal of toxic behavior patterns, and create this addiction to God.

Once again, salvation is a one-time occurrence, yet a continual process of working out your own salvation with fear and trembling, see Philippians 2:12. On the journey to spiritual maturity, the believer will experience multiple deliverances. The Holy Spirit's role in the process is to assist with the recovery of personality. In the book *Kingdom Within*, we find that "we are saved when the lost part of our personality is recovered, for this brings with it the King, the total person, the One in us who brings us joyfully into the kingdom of God."[154] Verse three of Isaiah chapter 53 describes the mystery of the secret identity between Savior and despised one; which depicts that personality and temperament are similar.

Regarding personality, John A. Sanford offers: "In this crisis of consciousness the personality must become new. The old personality simply cannot contain the new state of

---

[152] Sandford, John L., and Paula Sandford. *Healing the Wounded Spirit*. Victory House Publishers, 1985. 2.
[153] Leaf, Caroline. The Perfect You: A Blueprint for Identity. Ada: Baker Books, 2017. 53.
[154] Sanford, John A. The Kingdom Within: The Inner Meaning of Jesus' Sayings. HarperOne, 1987. 148.

consciousness that the kingdom demands from us. If the new personality is poured into the old framework, the old framework will burst asunder. The creative contents of the kingdom require a new and fresh consciousness to hold them ... The entrance to the kingdom is often a violent one, for entering into the kingdom means surrendering the old personality and finding a new wine. This new wine of a consciously lived life requires the new person. The new life is to be founded on the ethic of creative consciousness, and such a life is tremendously important to God himself."[155]

Tim LaHaye has written the best-selling classic *Spirit-Controlled Temperament – Who You Are And Who You Can Become* with the intent to help people understand how the Holy Spirit can enable believers to overcome weakness; which is NOT an automatic occurrence. A willing cooperation to the Spirit of God is required to produce a lasting change in life. This willingness of the spirit leads to the proper temperament that is needed to be successful in life.

"Temperament is a combination of traits we were born with; character is our 'civilized' temperament; and personality is the 'face' we show to others."[156] When people are unsure of their Imago Dei, the traits of anger and fear manifests. According to Tim LaHaye, "anger-related sins probably ruin more Christian testimonies than any other kind of sin."[157] He even goes further to identify sixteen manifestations of anger as: "Bitterness, malice, clamor, envy, resentment, intolerance, criticism, revenge, wrath, hatred, seditions, jealousy, attack, gossip, sarcasm, and unforgiveness."[158] Fear and anger are identified as universal sins, and LaHaye has additionally formulated a list of the various manifestations of fear as: "Anxiety, doubts,

---

[155] Sanford, John A. The Kingdom Within: The Inner Meaning of Jesus' Sayings. HarperOne, 1987. 53 and 57.
[156] Tim LaHaye. *Spirit-controlled Temperament*. (Carol Stream: Tyndale House Publishers, 1993). Xii, and 4.
[157] Ibid. 129.
[158] Ibid. 130

timidity, indecision, superstition, withdrawal, loneliness, over aggression, suspicion, hesitancy, depression, haughtiness, and social shyness."[159]

Allowing the Holy Spirit to dwell within gives Him access to control these manifestations of fear and anger. Galatians 5:22-23 describe the manifestation of the fruit of the spirit, which chokes out (starves) the works of the flesh and the carnal nature described earlier. Lastly, the Holy Spirit empowers believers to walk in forgiveness.

The love-hate relationship was discussed earlier in the distorted identity section. These must be healed and unraveled through a journey of forgiveness with the help of the Holy Spirit. "There is hope for change. But on the way to that hope is pain in breaking out of those old patterns that have locked in the love-hate dynamics. But once the decision is made to go through that painful experience, the love-hate foundation of fear, anger, and guilt can be destroyed and replaced with love, hope, joy, and freedom."[160]

Forgiveness

Forgiveness is a key to operating in the empowered identity. Several dimensions of forgiveness must be taken into account. Yes, to forgive others whom have caused hurt to us, but more importantly, to ask and seek forgiveness for our own misunderstanding of our Imago Dei – our true identity. Matthew 18:21-35 illustrates the parable of the unforgiving servant, or as The Passion Translation titles it: Unlimited Forgiveness. "And his master was angry, and

---

[159] Tim LaHaye. *Spirit-controlled Temperament*. (Carol Stream: Tyndale House Publishers, 1993). 147.
[160] Stephen Arterburn, and David A. Stoop. *When Someone You Love is Someone You Hate*. (W Publishing Group, 1988). 48.

delivered him to **the torturers** until he should pay all that was due to him (Matthew 18:34 NKJV, emphasis added)."

Bill Sudduth offers the following statement to illuminate the necessity of forgiveness in the life of believers: "The tormentors or torturers are demon spirits. They have a legal right to torment if you have unforgiveness. When we plant or water the seed of unforgiveness, bitterness will spring up. Bitterness has been defined as unfulfilled revenge."[161] This definition certainly makes it clear why forgiveness is needed, and at the same time, unforgiveness can be deemed as a powerful Screwtape Element to hinder the empowered identity.

"For **if you forgive people** their trespasses [their reckless and willful sins, leaving them, letting them go, and giving up resentment], your heavenly Father will also forgive you. But **if you do NOT forgive others** their trespasses [their reckless and willful sins, leaving them, letting them go, and giving up resentment], neither will your Father forgive you your trespasses (Matthew 6:14-15 AMPC, emphasis added)." Bill Sudduth offers the following checklist of what forgiveness is and isn't, which can be helpful with prompting believers to fully work through the layers of forgiveness.

"What Forgiveness is NOT:

1) Forgiveness is not saying that what a person did to you is OK.

    a) It is not OK. It will never be OK. It was wrong.

2) Forgiveness is not a feeling.

    a) It is obedience to God's Word.

---

[161] William Sudduth. *Deliverance Training Manual*. (RAM Inc., 2013). 23.

b) It is a choice. It's a decision to obey God.

3) Forgiveness is not healing.

a) Forgiveness paves the way or opens the door for healing.

b) If you have forgiven someone and still feel pain, it's because you need to receive your healing. The forgiveness comes first, then the healing.

"What Forgiveness IS:

1) Forgiveness is a command:

a) One of the biggest mistakes we could ever make is thinking forgiveness is an option. It is not an option, it is a commandment.

b) Unforgiveness is a sin issue.

2) Forgiveness is releasing them to God, it is turning them over to God."[162]

We are impelled to forgive, and we are commanded according to the following list of scriptures regarding key principles of forgiveness: Matthew 6:12-15; Luke 6:37-38; and Matthew 18:23-35. Therefore, "duty, responsibility, accountability, desire to please God, and desire to avoid not pleasing God motivate us to forgive."[163]

In the book *Caring For People God's Way*, the authors offer two ways to help people forgive: 1) through a psychoeducational group; 2) through couples therapy."[164] They also explain the difference between emotional forgiveness and decisional forgiveness. "*Emotional*

---

[162] William Sudduth. *Deliverance Training Manual*. (RAM Inc., 2013). 23.
[163] Tim Clinton, Archibald D. Hart, and George Ohlschlager. *Caring for People God's Way: Personal and Emotional Issues, Addictions, Grief, and Trauma*. (Nelson Reference & Electronic Publishing, 2005). 119.
[164] Ibid. 122.

forgiveness juxtaposes positive emotions toward the offender such as empathy, sympathy, compassion, agape love, or romantic love against the negative unforgiving emotions. Emotional forgiveness is born out of a valuing of the 'warmth-based virtues' [such as love, compassion, gratitude, humility, sympathy, and compassion] in contrast to the conscientiousness-based virtues that motivate decisional forgiving. The emotional juxtaposition first neutralizes negative emotions and second builds in positive emotions such as a net positive love, until emotional replacement occurs."[165]

Inner Healing

A Screwtape Element is to gain an understanding "that un-healed hurts hinder our Christian walk and the devil will use them to harm us or damage us and to slow us down."[166] Therefore, inner healing is necessary; which can be viewed as the childlike image depicted in Matthew 18:3-4. "This image is used by Jesus to represent our transformed personalities because of the child's freedom from any false, masklike front, which enables the child to remain spontaneous and creative. Until adults teach them differently, children reflect on the outside what they feel on the inside; there is as yet no split between appearance and reality. So the child remains in creative contact with the inner world; the ego and the unconscious are not split apart but have a natural and flowing relationship with each other. This is the relationship that members of the kingdom are to establish with their inner potentialities."[167] Thank God for the help of the Holy Spirit in the work of inner healing.

---

[165] Tim Clinton, Archibald D. Hart, and George Ohlschlager. *Caring for People God's Way: Personal and Emotional Issues, Addictions, Grief, and Trauma*. (Nelson Reference & Electronic Publishing, 2005). 122.
[166] William Sudduth. *Deliverance Training Manual*. (RAM Inc., 2013). 28.
[167] Sanford, John A. The Kingdom Within: The Inner Meaning of Jesus' Sayings. HarperOne, 1987. 37.

Inner healing is the process of allowing the Holy Spirit access into the wounds of the past. In essence, inner healing is cleaning the spiritual lenses of life that may have gotten filthy due to the past hurts and traumas in life. Salvation in Christ Jesus provided wholeness and entry from dark to light, see Colossians 1:12-14. Yet the added role of inner healing is to restore wholeness from all of the wounding that occurred in the darkness. The inner man can become captive to the distortions described in the previous chapter, and the lack of known identity. "Here are the steps someone must walk through to come out of captivity: 1) Repent of rebellious choices. 2) Accept forgiveness from God for burying self. 3) Renounce inner vows to disconnect from life. 4) Decide to stubbornly resist passivity."[168] These steps empower and free the personality of man.

"Inner healing involves going to the root of the problem and ministering healing. A past hurt or wound is like a sore on your body that just will not heal. It stays infected and festers, and at some point you have to scrub off the scab and clean it out. Then you can apply the salve and a clean bandage, and let it properly heal. This is binding up the brokenhearted."[169] Or, as Jesus describes His mission in Luke 4:18, to heal the brokenhearted: "The Spirit of the Lord is upon Me (the Messiah), because He has anointed Me to preach the good news to the poor. He has sent Me to announce release (pardon, forgiveness) to the captives, and recovery of sight to the blind, to set free those who are oppressed (downtrodden, bruised, crushed by tragedy) (Luke 4:18 AMPC)."

Another key factor to the empowered identity is a balanced diet. "The brain doesn't live by bread alone. In order to think, remember, or analyze, the brain needs more than

---

[168] Sandford, John L., and Paula Sandford. *Healing the Wounded Spirit*. Victory House Publishers, 1985. 69.
[169] William Sudduth. *Deliverance Training Manual*. (RAM Inc., 2013). 28.

glucose, it needs protein. This is because protein is required for the manufacture of certain key chemicals in the brain called neurotransmitters."[170] The brain also requires adamant amounts of water and vitamins to properly function. Dr. Daniel Amen has a series of books about *Change Your Brain, Change Your Life*, and *Change Your Brain, Change Your Body*. He describes *The Brain Warriors Way,* and how his clinic shares nine rules of brain-healthy eating to address these key factors.

> Summary Chart of the Amen Clinics 9 Rules of Brain-Healthy Eating
> Rule #1: Think "high-quality calories" and not too many of them.
> Rule #2: Drink plenty of water and not your calories.
> Rule #3: Eat high-quality lean protein throughout the day.
> Rule #4: Eat smart carbohydrates (low glycemic, high fiber).
> Rule #5: Focus your diet on healthy fats.
> Rule #6: Eat from the rainbow.
> Rule #7: Cook with brain-healthy herbs and spices to boost your brain.
> Rule #8: Make sure your food is as clean as possible.
> Rule #9: If you're having trouble with your mood, energy, memory, weight, blood sugar, blood pressure, or skin, make sure to eliminate any foods that might be causing trouble, especially wheat and any other gluten-containing grain or food, as well as dairy, soy, and corn.

[171]

The last concept to discuss regarding the empowered identity is the fact of the resiliency of human spirit that is recognized throughout life. Resilience is defined as: "an ability to recover from or adjust easily to misfortune or change. The capability of a strained body to recover its size and shape after deformation caused especially by compressive stress."[172] The goal of this project has been to empower believers and counselors to identify

---

[170] Reader's Digest. *ABC's of the Human Mind: A Family Answer Book*. (New York: Readers Digest, 1990). 82.
[171] Amen, Daniel G. *Change Your Brain, Change Your Life: The Breakthrough Program for Conquering Anxiety, Depression, Obsessiveness, Anger, and Impulsiveness*. (New York: Harmony, 2015). 384.
[172] Merriam Webster.

the misfortunes that have the capacity to deform identity, and assist in the recovery process of resiliency, as defined here.

CHAPTER SIX: Summary and Conclusions

In summary, Christian Counselors have been empowered with the tools of recognizing the dichotomy of identity and mental health issues. These tools assist counselors to identify identity breeches in their counselees and will help reduce mental health issues and be able to fulfill what Dr. Caroline Leaf has said: "Your purpose is to live beyond yourself through reflecting God's glory to a broken world."[173]

The foundation of righteousness is momentous to understanding the dichotomies discussed. It is interwoven throughout the understanding of the Community of God, the Imago Dei, the tri-part being of huMANkind, and the Screwtape Element. The ultimate priority is worship. Again, this is what the battle is all about. "Worship is not optional… In the grand scheme of redemption, one of the principle things God is doing is transforming sinners into worshippers."[174]

The statistics regarding mental health are staggering, yet understanable due to the illusory identity crises that many have experienced as a result of the carnal nature and distorted identity. Understanding the scientific workings of the brain throughout this process will prove beneficial to cleaning away the "stuff" that impairs the Imago Dei. Aftermath residue may manifest, such as a critical spirit, a codependent spirit, anxiety, depression, ADD, and addictions.

The empowered identity begins with recognizing and receiving salvation for the soul. "May we feel within us the eternal life of Jesus reaching through our hands – to heal, to hold,

---

[173] Leaf, Caroline. The Perfect You: A Blueprint for Identity. Ada: Baker Books, 2017. 285.

[174] John F. MacArthur *Worship: The Ultimate Priority*. (Chicago: Moody Publishers, 2012). 52.

to hug – and celebrate the bread of our Humanity, the sanctity of the Ordinary and Participation in the Trinity."[175] Yet there will be continued multiple deliverances throughout the remainder of life. The Holy Spirit plays a considerable role in the life of believers. It is through the power of the Holy Spirit that people are empowered to walk in forgiveness and receive inner healing. The prayers of the Lord Jesus Christ also equip believers to walk in this wholeness, and extend it to others, as in John 17:6-26. "His prayer is that the Imago Dei in each of us is so evident that the world cannot help but see His love."[176]

Ivory Hopkins offers several wisdom keys to Christian Counselors in his book titled *Who Counsels The Counselor*. In this manual, he shares principles of building and restoring leaders. The heart of counselors must regularly attain spiritual checkups while assisting others in the discovery of their Imago Dei, and deal with the various elements of distorted identity discussed in this research paper.

He states: "My purpose for writing this is to touch the hearts of the five-fold ministry gifts, I want to bless them and speak into their lives strength and courage. I ask that the Holy Spirit bring healing and counsel to those who minister to the body of Christ."[177] Two of the most helpful chapters in this book were 1) "What Leaders Should Do Before They Crash and Burn," and 2) "Wounded Leaders and How to Bounce Back." Counseling is most effective when the counselor has endeavored to seek personal healing by dealing with whatever issues

---

[175] Richard Rohr and Mike Morrell. *The Divine Dance: The Trinity and Your Transformation*. (Whitaker House, 2016. Kindle edition), 21.
[176] Catherine Skurja. *Paradox Lost: Uncovering the True Identity in Christ*. (Imago Dei Resources LLC, 2012). 194.
[177] Ivory Hopkins. *Who Counsels The Counselor: Building and Restoring Leaders*. (Scotts Valley: Createspace Independent Publishing Platform, 2019). 33.

are within the counselor, which will allow the counselor to be empowered to deal with whatever issues manifest in the counselees.

This process has been such an empowering journey that I have personally decided to fulfill a second Doctor of Philosophy in Christian Counseling with the thesis topic of: **THE DICHOTOMY OF RENEWAL OF THE MIND AND ADDICTIONS**. I have encountered far to much materials to incorporate into this manuscript, so I am already working on the next with a heart to bring healing to a generation of people that have been impacted by addictions in so many dimensions.

2nd Dichotomy

VOLUME TWO: THE DICHOTOMY OF RENEWAL OF THE MIND AND ADDICTIONS

Paulette Denise Turner

Newburgh Theological Seminary

Doctor of Philosophy in Christian Counseling

Specialization in Addiction Counseling

October 17, 2023

Dichotomy TWO: Dedication and Acknowledgments

I would like to dedicate this thesis project first and foremost to the Person of the Holy Spirit whom I now have access to through my Lord and Savior Jesus Christ. He is the greatest best Friend a person can have. Also, to all my family, friends, and loved ones who have overcome a multiplicity of addictions and life challenges through the Renewal Of The Mind.

Special acknowledgement goes to my husband, Pastor Don Turner, for your support while gathering this compilation of thoughts. Additionally, to my best friend Erica Shenise, yes you are my first-born daughter, but the Lord has given me a true gift in you now being an adult, girlfriend, and mentee. Lastly, to my Rakiya Shenell, you've blossomed so much since the last project, I'm looking forward to following your trajectory into womanhood.

Dichotomy TWO: Abstract

Background

Addictive behaviors are more than substance abuse, and can be of sex, gambling, people-pleasing, excessive internet usage, and more. An addiction is a repetitive habit that is harmful to a person's well-being. The Bible has a lot to say to counselors in compassionately assisting believers to renew their mind to be free from addictive mindsets, which lead to addictive behavior. Additionally, science and spirituality marry to make the renewal process complete.

Aim

The aim is to equip counselors and believers with a tool to excavate addictive mindsets and arrive at the authentic mind of Christ.

Methods

The most common method of research has been content analysis, along with inductive and deductive research.

Results

The results are a discipleship tool providing practical helpful strategies that can compassionately assist believers in the Renewal Of The Mind process and freedom from addictions. See the Appendix A worksheet.

Conclusions

The purpose is empowering believers with an understanding of the elements that need to be renewed in the mind to achieve freedom from addictions. This project is targeted to be for individuals, counselors, as well as to be used in group settings or counseling sessions to compassionately excavate roots and incorrect mindsets that enable addictions or addictive behavior.

Dichotomy TWO: Introduction

My previous dissertation addressed *The Dichotomy of Identity and Mental Health Issues*. This project will focus on the role and the "how to" of Renewing the Mind, to include processing feelings, understanding conscience, and healing from trauma in the process of being freed from addictions. The desired outcome is to develop a tool to be used for discipleship, instruction, deliverance, and a maturing understanding of salvation in the process of Renewal of the Mind and freedom from addictions.

A concept that was introduced in the first thesis is what I have termed the *Screwtape Element*, based loosely on C.S. Lewis's the Screwtape Letters. My summary of the Screwtape Element is to cause hu-MAN-kind, especially believers who have not thoroughly understood their Imago Dei (their identity in the Lord), to focus more on surface issues, and anything other than living as an upright citizen of the kingdom of God.

Defining Addictions

Identifying addictions is a complicated process because there is no single face of addiction, it is an equal opportunity situation. All ethnicities, age groups, and people are prone to addictive behaviors. Addiction is a vicious cycle that develops from multiple mechanisms including mental health stability, physical changes within the body, and the environment around one. An ongoing debate is whether addiction is a disease or a character flaw? Is addiction a function of the brain or the mind?

Once again, there is a huge debate as to whether addiction is a disease. The medical industry certainly agrees with this theory. However, it seems to be contrary in the life of believers. "Sadly, many believe that they have a disease that cannot be overcome. Mislabeling addiction hurts, not helps. Calling an addiction a disease is not wise because it often leads to blame-shifting."[178]

Addiction is NOT a brain disorder as some articles and books have alluded. The Bible discusses family propensity to have addictive behaviors in Ezekiel chapter 18. The medical field leans toward medicating the fruit, or symptoms of addiction, instead of exposing and dealing with the root causes of addictive behaviors. The question is not if addictive tendencies are genetically passed on, rather the fact that addictive tendencies are perpetuated through lifestyle choices, not genetics.

The real issue is that "at the heart of addiction is idolatry; therefore, we need heart surgery to remove the idol that has taken up residency. Psychologists are familiar with the term *cognitive dissonance*, which defines the battle inside a person who believes one way yet acts another. But God calls addiction *sin* and uses conviction to bring us in line with His truth."[179] Conversely, "the idol of addiction needs to be crushed, not coddled."[180] The idols need to be identified, not labeled as a disease.

Another term to define in the addiction process is *trigger*. "The term trigger refers to anything – an event, object, sound, smell, and so on – that activates the amygdala's alarm

---

[178] Idleman, Shane. *Help! I'm Addicted: Overcoming the Cravings that Overcome You*. El Paseo Publications, 2019. Kindle Edition. 31, 44, 40.

[179] Ibid.
[180] Ibid.

system as a result of association-based learning."[181] Some triggers cause emotional stability, or cognitive dissonance. Joyce Meyer addresses emotional stability in this manner: "I would like to deal specifically with what I call 'emotional addictions' and how to break them in order to enjoy emotional stability. In this context, an addiction can be defined as compulsory behavior, often in response to some stimulus, without conscious thought."[182]

The root of some of these triggers can be traced to childhood. "The deep pains of childhood can follow us, and the enemy of our soul will use them against us."[183] Shane Idleman states: "One of the greatest lessons I learned is that we can either fully yield to God or we can yield to sin. We are not robots on autopilot. We have been given the enormous responsibility of choice, and we must be accountable to our actions. We make a choice, then the choice makes us."[184] Once again, it is not a disease, but a choice.

Renew your mind that when an injustice is occurring, when a situation is happening that is contrary, instead of passively bowing out due to shame, embarrassment, or the confrontation of the situation you need to deal with it in your mind (in your thinking), whether you deal with it with the person or not. Basically, telling yourself one thing, and believing another is not good for your brain. You need to renew your mind with what is going on in your brain, you cannot internalize toxic feelings.

The mind must be renewed to how we handle triggers. Another term for this phenomenon is cognitive dissonance as mentioned above. "Active practice also has the

---

[181] Pittman, Catherine M., and Elizabeth M. Karle. *Rewire Your Anxious Brain: How to Use the Neuroscience of Fear to End Anxiety, Panic and Worry*. Oakland: New Harbinger Publications Inc, 2015. 45.
[182] Meyer, Joyce. *Beauty for Ashes: Receiving Emotional Healing*. Fenton: FaithWords, 2003. 168.
[183] Idleman, Shane. *Help! I'm Addicted: Overcoming the Cravings that Overcome You*. El Paseo Publications, 2019. Kindle Edition. 6.
[184] Ibid.

advantage of helping overcome cognitive dissonance, that uncomfortable feeling people often have when they understand and know something in their heads, but their feelings haven't yet caught up with their heads."[185]

Another aspect to take into consideration when defining addiction is *complacency*. Realizing that "complacency leads to apathy, and eventually, to compromise"[186] which "must be eradicated, not warmed. Removed, not welcomed."[187] These are all choices of the will which require emotional stability and a strong mind/soul. Lastly, the cost of addiction must be taken into consideration when defining addiction, it is much messier than initially viewed.

"The Cost of Addiction:

- Addiction hinders our relationship with God.
- Addiction turns into idolatry.
- Addiction damages our relationship with our spouse, children, family, and friends.
- Addiction fuels irritability and anger.
- Addiction leads to financial difficulty.
- Addiction hinders God's blessings."[188]

---

[185] Koch, Ruth N., and Kenneth C. Haugk. *Speaking the Truth in Love: How to be an Assertive Christian*. St Louis: Stephen Ministries St Louis, 1992. 184.
[186] Idleman, Shane. *Help! I'm Addicted: Overcoming the Cravings that Overcome You*. El Paseo Publications, 2019. Kindle Edition. 2, 24, 42-43.
[187] Ibid.
[188] Ibid.

PART ONE: DICHOTOMY RENEWAL OF THE MIND
CHAPTER SEVEN: The Realm Of The Mind

Renewal

The word of God is the basis for renewal. "To renew means to reestablish something after it has been interrupted or damaged."[189] This thesis is built upon two theme scriptures: Romans 12:1-2 and 1 Thessalonians 5:23.

- "So here's what I want you to do, God helping you: Take your everyday, ordinary life—your sleeping, eating, going-to-work, and walking-around life—and place it before God as an offering. Embracing what God does for you is the best thing you can do for him. Don't become so well-adjusted to your culture that you fit into it without even thinking. Instead, fix your attention on God. You'll be changed from the inside out. Readily recognize what He wants from you, and quickly respond to it. Unlike the culture around you, always dragging you down to its level of immaturity, God brings the best out of you, develops well-formed maturity in you (Romans 12:1-2 MSG)."

- "And may the God of peace Himself sanctify you through and through [separate you from profane things, make you pure and wholly consecrated to God]; and may your spirit <*pnuema*> and soul <*psuche*> and body <*soma*> be preserved sound and complete [and found] blameless at the coming of our Lord Jesus Christ (the Messiah) (1 Thessalonians 5:23 AMPC, *with interjections)*."

---

[189] Idleman, Shane. *Help! I'm Addicted: Overcoming the Cravings that Overcome You*. El Paseo Publications, 2019. Kindle Edition. 55.

The spirit of man is born mature at the new birth, it is the soul that must be renewed to receive from the spirit. Or another way of viewing this is that the lenses of the soul must be cleansed or corrected to rightly determine and make effective choices. Another term for *renewal* is *repentance* which "is a change of mind that leads to change in action."[190]

Mind/Soul

Psalm 131 references the Psalmist calming and quieting his soul to cease from fretting due to the fact hope is placed in the Lord forever. "The soul is often defined as the mind, will, and emotions. We see from this scripture that these areas may become addicted to certain types of behavior just as the body may become addicted to certain types of substances."[191] Hence, the mind, or soul, must be renewed to hope in the Lord.

Furthermore, "the word 'soul' as translated from Old Testament Hebrew means 'all of your thoughts, feelings, personality characteristics, self, desires, and passions.' The soul is who we are inside, from the top of our head to the bottom of our feet. The soul is felt and translated into action through the day-to-day function of the brain."[192] The brain is a part of the body, which should be viewed as "the servant of the mind."[193] The body is not irrelevant

---

[190] Idleman, Shane. *Help! I'm Addicted: Overcoming the Cravings that Overcome You*. El Paseo Publications, 2019. Kindle Edition. 45.

[191] Meyer, Joyce. *Beauty for Ashes: Receiving Emotional Healing*. Fenton: FaithWords, 2003. 173.

[192] Amen, Daniel. *Healing the Hardware of the Soul: Enhance Your Brain to Improve Your Work, Love, and Spiritual Life*. New York: Simon & Schuster, 2008. 5.

[193] Allen, James. *As a Man Thinketh*. Amazon, 2014. Kindle Edition. 33.

in the Renewal Of The Mind process because "a healthy soul actually enhances brain function, and a healthy brain is essential to a healthy soul."[194]

A healthy soul is cultivated by proper belief systems. "Man is buffeted by circumstances so long as he believes himself to be the creature of outside conditions, but when he realizes that he is a creative power, and that he may command the hidden soil and seeds of his being out of which circumstances grow, he then becomes the rightful master of himself."[195] Understanding the mind/soul is crucial. The following quote from Lester Sumerall sums up the importance: "The strongest force you have is your mind – so Satan will come against it because that is where decisions are made. God and the devil both appeal for the attention of the mind (thoughts) – the battle is for the mind."[196]

The word mind is part of the psuche, which is "translated as: heart, life, soul, self, and MIND. This is the basis of some English words such as psychology, psychological, etc."[197] The following table was adapted mostly from a class I attended while at Rhema Bible Training College:

---

[194] Amen, Daniel. *Healing the Hardware of the Soul: Enhance Your Brain to Improve Your Work, Love, and Spiritual Life*. New York: Simon & Schuster, 2008. 6. Allen, James. *As a Man Thinketh*. Amazon, 2014. Kindle Edition. 10.

[195] Allen, James. *As a Man Thinketh*. Amazon, 2014. Kindle Edition. 10.

[196] Beaty, Cooper. "Lesson 5." Lecture, Principles of Learning And Teaching Methods, Rhema Bible Training College, Broken Arrow, OK, September 29, 2003.

[197] Beaty, Cooper. "Lesson 4." Lecture, Principles of Learning And Teaching Methods, Rhema Bible Training College, Broken Arrow, OK, September 19, 2003.

Spirit – Pneuma – 4151	Soul – Psuche – 5590	Body – Soma – 4983
MUST BE BORN AGAIN	MUST BE RENEWED	MUST BE MORTIFIED
Intuition; communion with God	Intellect; feelings; emotions; affections; desires; sentiments; will (power to choose)	
Conscience (the voice of the human spirit)	Reason (the voice of the soul)	Feelings (the voice of the body)
BECOME GOD-CONSCIOUS	BECOME SELF-CONSCIOUS	BECOME WORLD-CONSCIOUS

"Feelings are the connecting link between what we know (intellect) and what we do (will). However, the feelings can be controlled. We can CHOOSE the direction these point."[198] Cooper Beaty further illustrated the role of intellect, sensibilities, and the will as the power to know according to 1 Corinthians 2:9-16. Demonstrated further by this table:

INTELLECT: What we know…	SENSIBILITIES: What we feel…	WILL: What we do…

Lastly, Bill Gillham views the soul of man as the following "three component parts:

MIND – Your Thinker	WILL – Your Chooser	EMOTIONS: Your Feeler."[199]

---

[198] Beaty, Cooper. "Lesson 7." Lecture, Principles of Learning And Teaching Methods, Rhema Bible Training College, Broken Arrow, OK, October 8, 2003.

[199] Gillham, Bill. *Lifetime Guarantee*. Eugene: Harvest House Pub, 1993. 75.

Early Formation

This section will navigate through numerous ideas related to human needs and basic rights. These needs not being met, especially in childhood, are open doors and entryways for addictions to manifest and can damage the conscience.

Gary Chapman defines the basic needs of mankind like this: "Our Basic Needs: **Love – Freedom – Significance – Recreation – Peace with God**."[200] He details further regarding this list of needs, inner drives, and desires that prompt behaviors:

- The need for love: this is fundamental and the opposite of loneliness. Both positive and negative behavior is influenced by our need for love.

- The need for freedom: not to be controlled by others. Often the need for love and freedom are in conflict. Therefore, give and take is required to balance these two needs. Dr. Chapman says that "when your spouse angrily accuses you of trying to control his behavior, he is giving you a clue as to what motivates such inappropriate behavior – a need for freedom."[201] Yet maturity in marriage is demonstrated by both spouses learning to meet the needs of each other in wholesome ways.

- The need for significance: the quest for altruism. This need often motivates the workaholic or perfectionist.

---

[200] Chapman, Gary D. *Desperate Marriages: Moving Toward Hope and Healing in Your Relationship*. Chicago: Northfield Pub, 2008. 50, 56.
[201] Ibid.

- The need for recreation: finding ways to relax and maintain inner psychological equilibrium.
- The need for peace with God: while many people have spurned religion, the quest for spiritual reality has continued to motivate human behavior. "We all have a spiritual hunger that impels us to seek meaning beyond the world of food, sex, and activities."[202]

June Hunt refers to understanding the inner needs as follows: "In reality, we have all been created with three God-Given Inner Needs:

- **Love** – to know that someone is unconditionally committed to our best interest. John 15:12
- **Significance** – to know that our lives have meaning and purpose. Psalm 57:2
- **Security** – to feel accepted and a sense of belonging. Proverbs 14:26."[203]

The book *Speaking The Truth In Love* lists the following basic human rights:

- "Each person has the right to be treated respectfully.
- Each person has the right to say no without explanation and without guilt.
- Each person has the right to slow down and take time to think.
- Each person has the right to change his or her mind.

---

[202] Chapman, Gary D. *Desperate Marriages: Moving Toward Hope and Healing in Your Relationship.* Chicago: Northfield Pub, 2008. 49

[203] Hunt, June. *Guilt: Living Guilt-Free.* Peabody: Aspire Press, 2013. 54-55.

- Each person has the right to ask for what he or she wants.
- Each person has the right to ask for information.
- Each person has the right to make mistakes.
- Each person has the right to make choices and accept the consequences of those choices.
- Each person has the right to own and express his or her own feelings.
- Each person has the right to ask for help.
- Each person has the right to maintain a separate self that is accountable to God and independent of the expectations, the approval, or the influence of others."[204]

Some of the primary reasons of addiction stem from a lack of understanding of these fundamental human rights and needs. In the book *Lifetime Guarantee* Bill Gillham states that in reality, "you have the same rights Jesus had when He left heaven and came to earth: NONE. You are a *living sacrifice*. You are to *seek God first* and He will supply all your *needs*."[205] This is an active interpretation of an amalgamation of Romans 12:1, Matthew 6:33, and Philippians 4:19.

The Screwtape Element is that we have been violated and therefore have a skewed view of our human rights; and need to Renew our Mind to what our heavenly rights are. "If you have been violated through abuse, your rights as a human being were dishonored, which

---

[204] Koch, Ruth N., and Kenneth C. Haugk. *Speaking the Truth in Love: How to be an Assertive Christian*. St Louis: Stephen Ministries St Louis, 1992. 199.

[205] Gillham, Bill. *Lifetime Guarantee*. Eugene: Harvest House Pub, 1993. 172.

can cause you to feel overwhelmed. Those of us who grew up in a dysfunctional home are often so insecure that we create dysfunctional homes too."[206]

Conscience vs. Conscious

There is a difference between conscience and conscious. Conscious is one's awareness of self and the world around them, their place in the world. Conscience is one's ability to distinguish between what is right and what is wrong, what is morally and socially acceptable. When considering these two concepts, just remember that conscious means to be *awake and aware*, while conscience refers to *your inner sense of right and wrong*: the inner universe. Additionally, conscience can be defined as "the mind's sense of obligation to do what is believed to be right and not do what is believed to be wrong."[207]

Let's begin this section with a scripture that showcases the distinction between the mind and conscience, and how they can be corrupted. "To the pure [in heart and **conscience**] all things are pure, but to the defiled and corrupt and unbelieving nothing is pure; *their very minds and consciences* are defiled and polluted (Titus 1:15 AMPC, emphasis added)" The conscience is the compass in the moral world. Yet, there is also the conscious.

The word conscious is not in the New King James version (NKJV) or Modern English version (MEV) of the Bible. However, the Amplified Classic version (AMPC) uses it several

---

[206] Meyer, Joyce. *Beauty for Ashes: Receiving Emotional Healing*. Fenton: FaithWords, 2003. 218.
[207] Beaty, Cooper. "Lesson 11." Lecture, Principles of Learning And Teaching Methods, Rhema Bible Training College, Broken Arrow, OK, October 22, 2003.

times as descriptive and amplifying words comparable to a portion of the definition of the word *righteousness*. Reading and meditating on the following scriptures will allow one to be aware of the implication of conscience and conscious:

- "And if it were true that I have erred, my error would remain with me [I would be **conscious** of it] (Job 19:4 AMPC)."
- "Therefore, being **conscious** of fearing the Lord with respect and reverence, we seek to win people over [to persuade them]. But what sort of persons we are is plainly recognized and thoroughly understood by God, and I hope that it is plainly recognized and thoroughly understood also by your **consciences** (your inborn discernment) (2 Corinthians 5:11 AMPC)."
    - o Inborn discernment, discerning of spirits, recognizing what is of God, and what is not of God (not discerning of people), but of the spirit realm. You renew your mind to mature in your capacity to discern what is of God, and what is not of God.
- "The Lord rewarded me according to my righteousness (my **conscious** integrity and sincerity with Him); according to the cleanness of my hands has He recompensed me (Psalm 18:20 AMPC)."
    - o When we know we are walking in integrity with God; and when we understand that our conscious and our conscience must be aligned with the Tree of Life is when we get recompensed for the work of our hands.
- "For I am **conscious** of my transgressions and I acknowledge them; my sin is ever before me (Psalm 51:3 AMPC)."

- - Be made aware of your transgressions. Like when Ezra the scribe stood and read the word of God, the children of Israel became aware of their sin (transgressions) and repented. When you are empowered by the Holy Spirit you will walk in repentance instead of condemnation.
- "We have renounced disgraceful ways (secret thoughts, feelings, desires and underhandedness, the methods and arts that men hide through shame); we refuse to deal craftily (to practice trickery and cunning) or to adulterate or handle dishonestly the Word of God, but we state the truth openly (clearly and candidly). And so we commend ourselves in the sight and presence of God to every man's **conscience** (2 Corinthians 4:2 AMPC)."

Another way to view the word conscience is to literally see it as Con-science. The word science is highly related to knowledge. Hence, the word con-science can be interpreted as *with knowledge*. Believers need revelation knowledge to not allow erroneous knowledge to mislead them. Watchman Nee was heard to say: "all knowledge is the outgrowth of obedience; everything else is just information." Therefore, the truths revealed in this project will remain *just information* if not converted to *knowledge* through *obedience*.[208]

The same Greek word for conscience is used in the following three scriptures, as well as it is used thirty-two times in the New Testament, deriving from the root word meaning co-perception.[209] Conscience can be observed to be *in the state of clean or clear*. Additionally, the blood of Jesus cleanses and purifies one's conscience.

---

[208] Gillham, Bill. *Lifetime Guarantee*. Eugene: Harvest House Pub, 1993. 141.

[209] Bible Search and Study Tools - Blue Letter Bible. Accessed July 26, 2023. https://www.blueletterbible.org/.

- "Holding fast to faith (that leaning of the entire human personality on God in absolute trust and confidence) and having a good (clear) **conscience**. By rejecting and thrusting from them [**their conscience**], some individuals have made shipwreck of their faith (1 Timothy 1:19 AMPC)."

- "[And see to it that] **your conscience** is entirely clear (unimpaired), so that, when you are falsely accused as evildoers, those who threaten you abusively and revile your right behavior in Christ may come to be ashamed [of slandering your good lives]. (1 Peter 3:16 AMPC)."

- "How much more surely shall the blood of Christ, Who by virtue of [His] eternal Spirit [His own preexistent divine personality] has offered Himself as an unblemished sacrifice to God, purify **our consciences** from dead works and lifeless observances to serve the [ever] living God? (Hebrews 9:14 AMPC)."

- "I am speaking the truth in Christ. I am not lying; **my conscience** [enlightened and prompted] by the Holy Spirit bearing witness with me that I have bitter grief and incessant anguish in my heart (Romans 9:1-2 AMPC, emphasis added)."
  - The Passion Translation states this portion as "**My conscience** will not let me speak anything but the truth (Romans 9:1b, TPT)."

Gregg Braden discusses the conditions of the conscious as follows: "It's our ability to purposefully create the conditions of consciousness (thoughts, feelings, emotions, and beliefs) that lock one possibility of our choosing into the reality of our lives. And this is what brings science full circle with the world's ancient spiritual traditions. Both science and mysticism describe a force that connects everything together and gives us the power to influence how matter behaves – and reality itself – simply through the way we perceive the world around us."[210]

There are several categorizations of the conscience which "is usually helpful, but since it can be so easily distorted and is merely a reflection of an internalized set of values which have been *learned* we need to be cautious."[211] Once again, the conscience can easily be distorted, therefore it is helpful to become familiar with the following categories of the conscience.

"Categories of Conscience:

- Cognitive – insightful, Romans 12:2

- Convicting – ethical, Romans 2:15

- Cleansed – purified, Hebrews 9:14

- Clear – confident, 1 Peter 3:1

- Corrupt – impure, Titus 1:15

- Calloused – seared, 1 Timothy 4:2."[212]

---

[210] Braden, Gregg. *The Divine Matrix: Bridging Time, Space, Miracles, and Belief*. Carlsbad: Hay House, 2007. 78.
[211] Hart, Archibald D. *Unlocking the Mystery of Your Emotions*. W Publishing Group, 1989. 115.
[212] Hunt, June. *Guilt: Living Guilt-Free*. Peabody: Aspire Press, 2013. 46-47.

Furthermore, "in Christian circles there are three important determiners of an aggravated conscience. These are:

1) An inadequate God concept.

2) An inadequate sin concept.

3) An inadequate forgiveness concept."[213]

Regarding this third determiner Dr. Hart further states: "Forgiveness is the genius of Christianity. It is the heart of the gospel – and the essence of Christ's substitutionary death on the cross. No other religious belief system places it as central as the gospel does."[214] Proving that forgiveness is a profound element of a clear and clean conscience.

Another aspect to take into consideration when viewing both the conscious and conscience is that of the two trees in the garden of Eden: 1) the tree of life, and 2) the tree of the knowledge of good and evil. Jesus Christ is the Tree of Life. Believers must allow the Tree of Life, Jesus, to shape their conscience and not "knowledge" apart from Him.

However, the conscious awareness of mankind was awakened when mankind partook of the tree of the knowledge of good and evil. This brought forth disobedience, which was to rely on the promise of "knowledge" instead of God. Prior to the deception of Genesis chapter three, their conscious awareness was of their connection and relationship to God, they had regular communion with Him. When their conscious was awakened to know good and evil, their conscience was quickened, but separated from God.

---

[213] Hart, Archibald D. *Unlocking the Mystery of Your Emotions*. W Publishing Group, 1989. 120, 121-122.
[214] Ibid.

Believers must beware of compromising their conscience for a momentary convenience, a good conscience must have the TRUTH for a standard. It is the truth that will set one free from the lies that have been believed and from addictions. Convictions must be based on right beliefs if the conscience is to be a safe guide. Right beliefs are rooted in the tree of Life which is formed by the Renewal Of The Mind. Let this mind be in you. We have the mind of Christ according to Philippians 2:5 and 1 Corinthians 2:16. One cannot allow culture to shape their conscience; it must be rooted and grounded from above: in the mind of Christ and in the word of God.

The conscience can be seared through repeated drug abuse or addictions. When this occurs, one may have behaviors resembling that of a psychopath, unable to feel and acknowledge the needed remorse to renew the mind, to change. Yet another issue that has occurred with the conscience is that religious leaders have attempted to control the consciences of believers, instead of allowing them to develop their own beliefs, or assisting in building proper beliefs.

Guilt

Not all guilt is bad. June Hunt shares that at times "God intends to use the conviction of your guilt to lead you to confession and repentance so that He might have a restored relationship with you."[215] Another author develops this concept further by stating that "Guilt

---

[215] Hunt, June. *Guilt: Living Guilt-Free*. Peabody: Aspire Press, 2013. 50.

is designed to correct behavior, not punish it; to bring us to repentance, not send us to hell. Guilt should serve as a warning sign that something is wrong – not as self-punishment."[216]

However, the incorrect way to process guilt is as "a self-imposed prison when granted residence in you."[217] Instead, one should allow guilt to lead to repentance, and a restored relationship with God. Shane Idleman agrees by sharing that "the guilt, fear, and conviction we can feel are used by God to draw us to repentance and are wholly appropriate."[218]

Yet "of all the emotions, guilt must be the one with the most overlap between psychology and theology. Psychological guilt is a *feeling* or *emotion*. Spiritual or theological guilt is a *state of being*."[219] Once again, the purpose of guilt should be to expose areas that need repentance, not to gain an identity from those areas, which can lead to bondage to emotions or toxic behaviors such as addiction.

We discussed the role of the conscience in the previous section. Note that "there are differences between a demanding conscience and having a guilt that is neurotic in the degree and quality of the tension it produces. Your guilt can be labeled as neurotic when it has the following qualities:

- You have a strong sense of your own evil.
- You feel guilty nearly all the time without adequate justification.
- You keep labeling yourself as *bad*.
- Your guilt reactions last a long time.

---

[216] Hart, Archibald D. *Unlocking the Mystery of Your Emotions*. W Publishing Group, 1989. 117.
[217] Hunt, June. *Guilt: Living Guilt-Free*. Peabody: Aspire Press, 2013. 89.
[218] Idleman, Shane. *Help! I'm Addicted: Overcoming the Cravings that Overcome You*. El Paseo Publications, 2019. Kindle Edition. 44.
[219] Hart, Archibald D. *Unlocking the Mystery of Your Emotions*. W Publishing Group, 1989. 109.

- Your guilt is triggered by imagined wrongs, and then you cannot stop the guilt.
- Your guilt so incapacitates you that you cannot relate to anyone and want to withdraw.
- Your guilt causes you to want to take extreme actions (such as suicide) to remedy your wrongs.
- You cannot stop remembering all your past misdeeds."[220]

Once again, "God uses guilt to get our attention, but He never designed guilt to distress us forever. God created guilt to prick a calloused conscience, to move us to repent, to convict us of our wrong, and to convince us to do right."[221] The purpose of guilt is for believers to become aware of sin in their lives and gain freedom over sin through identity in Christ to fulfill His plan to restore His image in us, to adjust our attitudes and actions.

There is another aspect of guilt to consider: that is the difference between false and true guilt. "False guilt arises when you blame yourself even though you've committed no wrong or after having done something wrong, you've confessed and turned from your sin. False guilt keeps you in bondage to three destructive masters: shame, fear, and anger. False guilt, ironically, is not resolved by confession because, as a factual matter, there is nothing to confess. Confession won't be effective because false guilt is not based on truth but rather a lie."[222]

---

[220] Hart, Archibald D. *Unlocking the Mystery of Your Emotions*. W Publishing Group, 1989. 118.
[221] Hunt, June. *Guilt: Living Guilt-Free*. Peabody: Aspire Press, 2013. 8, 14.
[222] Ibid.

Contrasted to *true guilt* which shows us where we have erred and where we need to change, true guilt is the appropriate response and what we should feel when we have sinned. This type of guilt motivates, pushes, and prods us to be all that God created us to be. It is healthy and helpful in the Renewal Of The Mind process. As in Matthew 11:28-30, when the feeling of being heavy burdened with guilt arises, the choice is to *come unto Jesus* and learn of Him.

We will discuss feelings in depth in another section, for now know that "the root cause of false guilt is based on inaccurate feelings that have taken control of our thought process. These thinking patterns, and ultimately our major belief system, damage our concept of God and camouflage our need for a Savior."[223] Another author expounds on the connection of false guilt which is a result of the lies believed through the emotions. He says: "false guilt *feels* exactly like valid guilt (a conviction from the Holy Spirit). You can't tell the difference by how they *feel*. Your feeler will return the same verdict for both. Guilty! The jury is fixed as far as the feeler is concerned."[224]

Shame is another feeling that must be delineated when it concerns dealing with guilt. "Most people assume that *guilt* and *shame* are basically the same. However, guilt focuses on *what we've done* while shame focuses on *who we are*."[225] Identity is in Christ Jesus, which is who we are; identity is not based on anything that we've done.

---

[223] Hunt, June. *Guilt: Living Guilt-Free*. Peabody: Aspire Press, 2013. 57.

[224] Gillham, Bill. *Lifetime Guarantee*. Eugene: Harvest House Pub, 1993. 29.

[225] Hunt, June. *Guilt: Living Guilt-Free*. Peabody: Aspire Press, 2013. 22.

Hence, the need to discover the source of guilt. "Though we may not be aware of it, in the deepest part of our being, we can function on the basis of buried, negative beliefs about ourselves. These beliefs become the basis for our behaviors and the dictator of our decisions. Based on these unique roles, consider the following buried beliefs that can be clues to unresolved feelings of guilt even within ourselves!"[226] These two concepts can be useful in unearthing skewed belief systems that are producing guilt:

- "Discern if my guilty feelings are related to rules and regulations from childhood, church, or culture.
- Determine if my guilt is the result of failing to meet God's, someone else's, or my own expectations of me."[227]

Subconscious

The subconscious mind can be viewed like a bookshelf or a computer that stores information. Every life experience and encounter is stored in the subconscious mind. The word sub-conscious has the beginning of the word being *sub*, which is like saying beneath the surface, like a submarine.

---

[226] Hunt, June. *Guilt: Living Guilt-Free*. Peabody: Aspire Press, 2013. 30-31, 70.

[227] Ibid.

The following illustration depicts the iceberg concept of the conscience and subconscious mind. Many memories are trapped in the subconscious mind that trigger different thoughts and even physical symptoms in the body. Memories will be addressed further in a later section, for now, just know that what is not revealed cannot be healed; the concealed must be revealed.

This graphic was created to visually explain the dimensions of the conscious and subconscious mind, and the realms of thought and memory.

To discover concealed memories, one could ask the question "What are the negative attributes of your childhood?" The unconscious, or subconsciousness were being formed during childhood and can be root causes of addictions. These toxic memory structures must be dismantled.

Better yet, "the point here is to demonstrate the similarities and interchangeability of the subconscious, mind, and heart. Imagine your thought life changing because you simply became more attuned to your subconscious, internal, inmost, repressed, or mental self."[228] Gayle Rogers shared the following which enforces the need to understand what is happening in the subconscious mind: "I have assessed that if a person is untrained in how to listen effectively and if their perception is imbalanced by hurts, disappointments, distrust of people and other toxic poisonings, no matter how hard one tries to communicate, that person will only hear what their programmed subconscious mind will allow them to hear."[229]

The Thought Life And Strongholds

The thought life is so important because this is where beliefs are formed. According to 2 Corinthians 10:4-5, it is the location of warfare whereby thoughts must be in alignment with the mind of Christ. This is subsequently illustrated in Proverbs chapter one. "Pay close attention, my child, to your father's wise words and never forget your mother's instructions. For their insight will bring you success, adorning you with *grace-filled thoughts* and giving you reins to guide your decisions (Proverbs 1:8-9 TPT, emphasis added)." The Amplified version of this verse nine refers to the parental instructions as being *grace upon one's head and neck*; these are the physical regions of the thought life.

---

[228] Rogers, Gayle. *Healing The Traumatized Soul*. AuthorHouse, 2005. 75.
[229] Ibid. 130.

The book of Proverbs again states that as a man thinks, so he is; and James Allen adds "as he continues to think, so he remains."[230] It is as one changes their thoughts, their life changes. A healthy thought life changes the way we pray and speak regularly. Therefore, one must change what we are ruminating on inwardly, below the surface, in the subconscious mind. Purify this to find an active life, manifesting purity.

The thought life must be purged of "thoughts of malice, envy, disappointment, despondency, which rob the body of its health and grace."[231] Health and grace must be the focus of thoughts. Such selfless thoughts are the very avenues to heaven; and to reside day by day in thoughts of peace toward every creature will provide abounding peace to their owner. To think respectfully of all, to be cheerful with all, and gradually come to recognize the good in all. "Man's mind may be likened to a garden, which may be intelligently cultivated or allowed to run wild; but whether cultivated or neglected, it must, and will, *bring forth*."[232]

The Apostle Paul stimulates believers in Philippians chapter four to think on things from above, on higher thoughts rather than selfish thoughts knowing that the thought life is an entryway to strongholds being formed. This process, according to another author, looks like this: "Don't give the adversary room to work in your life! Change how you think. Thoughts are like strongholds that are built up within us, and if we build our inner 'house' out of thoughts that do not align with God's Word, we are aligning ourselves with darkness and inviting the enemy to bring confusion and weakness into our thought patterns."[233]

---

[230] Allen, James. *As a Man Thinketh*. Amazon, 2014. Kindle Edition. 25.
[231] Ibid. 20, 9.

[232] Ibid.

[233] Stearns, Robert. *The Cry of Mordecai: Awakening an Esther Generation in a Haman Age*. Shippensburg: Destiny Image Pub, 2009. 53.

These areas of confusion and weakness are often formed early in life. "Inner vows made in childhood may be at the root of some addictive issues. Formative years set the shape of our character. Inner vows are usually made before teen years, and then forgotten. Having more power by their subliminal (below the light of consciousness) and invisible nature. Suspect the presence of an inner vow when counseling and prayer do not produce changes. Begin to ask questions and be patient, asking questions activates the mnemonic device, a memory recall system. Therefore, asking questions can prime the well of memories and reveal inner vows."[234]

Strongholds can be described as a mental house made of thoughts at an early age for future occupation of spiritual forces, either godly or evil. "They help to contrast those beliefs that can be empirically demonstrated (rational) with those that have no substantiation whatsoever (irrational). These irrational beliefs give rise to irrational thoughts which are then followed by illogical thinking. When this occurs with deeply personal matters, the emotional consequences can be disastrous."[235] Resulting in lifelong strongholds if not addressed.

Archibald Hart likewise clarifies irrational thought patterns as: "these distorted beliefs are acquired in childhood, and they don't grow up with us. We become adult but our beliefs remain childish. We then perpetuate them throughout our lives by failing to challenge or dispose of them. We only become aware of these irrational beliefs after we have suffered from their consequences. Seldom can we recognize them before they get us into emotional

---

[234] Hart, Archibald D. *Unlocking the Mystery of Your Emotions*. W Publishing Group, 1989. 30, 31.

[235] Ibid.

trouble."[236] Hence, the need to understand the early formation of belief systems, and the renewal of them through removing the hidden strongholds.

"It is tremendously important that we understand where the battle is taking place. The Apostle Paul used various words to speak of the battleground and our objectives. I compiled the following list of words from different translations: imaginations, reasonings, speculations, arguments, knowledge, and thought. Notice that every one of these words refers to the same realm, the realm of the mind. We absolutely must understand that the battleground is in the realm of the mind. Satan is waging an all-out war to captivate the minds of humanity. He is building strongholds and fortresses in their minds, and it is our responsibility, as God's representatives, to use our spiritual weapons to break down these strongholds, to liberate the minds of men and women, and then to bring them into captivity to the obedience of Christ. What a staggering assignment that is! Satan deliberately and systematically builds strongholds in people's minds."[237]

Regarding strongholds and addictions, we must comprehend that "at the heart of addiction rests a common denominator known as a stronghold. Addiction truly is hell on earth – you're enslaved but desperately want freedom, you're bound but can't break free, you're in tremendous pain but can't find relief. If you can relate, don't worry, there is hope."[238] Another building block for addictive strongholds is *pride*, which needs to be destroyed. Honesty, openness, morality, and disclosure are necessary in the destruction of the stronghold of pride.

---

[236] Ibid.

[237] Prince, Derek. *Spiritual Warfare*. Charlotte: Whitaker House, 2001. 35.

[238] Idleman, Shane. *Help! I'm Addicted: Overcoming the Cravings that Overcome You*. El Paseo Publications, 2019. Kindle Edition. 1.

The Bible indicates two kinds of strongholds in people's minds: "These are prejudices and preconception."[239] Both of these can be toxic in the thought life and must be renewed. "The exciting news is that you are not stuck with the brain that you have; brain problems can be improved and even healed,"[240] providing new thinking and hope in the destruction of strongholds.

Derek Prince offers the following regarding strongholds and prayer: "Somewhere between God's heavenly domain and us is a hostile kingdom that opposes us and seeks to hinder our prayers. And that is why we sometimes have to push through enemy territory when we pray. It is not that we are praying out of the will of God, or that God is unwilling to hear us, but that we have to penetrate a hostile kingdom in the heavenlies in order to reach Him."[241] There is an obstructing kingdom. "Jesus ascended far above Satan's kingdom, but Satan's kingdom remained in place."[242] These strongholds must be abolished.

There are individual as well as ancestorial strongholds that must be spiritually dismantled. The Bible talks about being slaves to God, no longer to sin in Romans chapter six. Spiritually speaking, many have been given the legacy and example of being slaves to sin. However, Derek Prince addresses both the physical and spiritual ramifications of slavery: "My opinion is that if your ancestor was a slave, you may have been politically emancipated, but if you have never been spiritually emancipated, you will remain under a spirit of slavery. My observation is that many African Americans battle with legalism; they struggle to know the

---

[239] Prince, Derek. *Spiritual Warfare*. Charlotte: Whitaker House, 2001. 36.

[240] Amen, Daniel. *Healing the Hardware of the Soul: Enhance Your Brain to Improve Your Work, Love, and Spiritual Life*. New York: Simon & Schuster, 2008. 16.

[241] Prince, Derek. *Pulling Down Strongholds*. Charlotte: Whitaker House, 2013. 23, 26, 28.

[242] Ibid.

real liberty of God's grace. The reason is that the spirit of slavery has not been fully dealt with, and it still has a measure of control over them. As a group, they have never been set free, spiritually."[243]

The thought life is crucial and must be stimulated. Derek Prince went on to say: "If the church would only start *thinking*, we could not be defeated. It has always impressed me that Martin Luther started the Protestant Reformation by pinning up the ninety-five theses on the church door at Wittenberg. He couldn't pin up all the answers – he just got everyone to *start thinking*. When they started thinking, things changed. That is how important it is for us to learn to think"[244] and the significance of understanding the thought life.

The following points must be addressed when dealing with strongholds:

1. "Remove excuses.

2. Avoid triggers.

3. Own it and repent.

4. Apologize and repair the damage.

5. Crush pride before it crushes you.

6. Don't entertain compromise.

7. Admit your dependence on God, and fully surrender to Him."[245]

---

[243] Ibid.

[244] Prince, Derek. *Spiritual Warfare*. Charlotte: Whitaker House, 2001. 41.

[245] Idleman, Shane. *Help! I'm Addicted: Overcoming the Cravings that Overcome You*. El Paseo Publications, 2019. Kindle Edition. 4.

Feelings And Emotions

Thoughts and feelings are not the same thing; feelings can be the result of thoughts. "This emphasis, which stresses the relation between our thoughts (cognitions) and our emotions (affect), has recently been receiving renewed interest in psychotherapy."[246] Archibald Hart says that "feelings are our friends, and they should neither imprison us nor be imprisoned by us. Knowing how to experience them, own up to them, and even control them when necessary is essential to mental and spiritual health – and to emotional freedom."[247]

James Allen puts it this way: "Man is made or unmade by himself; in the armory of thought he forges the weapons, by which he destroys himself; he also fashions the tools with which he builds for himself heavenly mansions of joy and strength and peace."[248]

Bill Gillham says that the role of feelings must be understood because "feelings are wonderful when they line up with *God's* reality. The problem is that they also react to earthly circumstances. This is when you are most highly motivated to *walk after the flesh* rather than to walk in the finished work of Christ *for* you *in* the circumstance."[249]

While discussing mental armory, John Gray shared the following about how he was unmade by the wounds in his soul: "Every decade or so the bandage would give out, oozing

---

[246] Hart, Archibald D. *Unlocking the Mystery of Your Emotions*. W Publishing Group, 1989. 6, 159.

[247] Ibid.

[248] Allen, James. *As a Man Thinketh*. Amazon, 2014. Kindle Edition. 7.
[249] Gillham, Bill. *Lifetime Guarantee*. Eugene: Harvest House Pub, 1993. 17.

the contents of the infected wound – my soul – everywhere, until I managed to replace the bandage again and get it under control."[250]

Gayle Rogers describes in depth the wound process. "The word *wound* is also the root word for bruised, transliterated as *tramata* or trauma. Given these definitions, it is not difficult to understand why so many people have damaged emotions resulting in unresolved issues often hidden in the little black box that Reneisa Martin talks about. My intent throughout this book, in addition to describing how memories, thoughts, and emotions are hidden in the subconscious mind, eventually becoming contaminated over time, is to teach you of the power we have to literally heal yourself from these toxic, contaminated memories and emotions. The more you study to gain understanding of the mind-body-brain functioning, the more you understand your God-given power within your DNA."[251]

Each of us has a magnificent creation inside of us that we may bring into the world. Nelson Brady reinforces this concept and adds an additional terminology to explain the phenomenon. "It's different for every person. And it all boils down to what is called *the heart wall*."[252] One's capacity to love others and oneself is hampered by the heart wall. "Love is an energy that passes from you to another person. It interferes with your ability to receive love and to feel good emotions. It contributes to feelings of isolation and can create depression."[253] Depression transpires when the most fundamental aspect of us, "our heart, our core, is

---

[250] Amen, Tana. *The Relentless Courage of a Scared Child: How Persistence, Grit, and Faith Created a Reluctant Healer*. Nashville: Thomas Nelson, 2021. 161.

[251] Rogers, Gayle. *The Whole Soul: Rescripting Your Life for Personal Transformation*. Kingdom House Publishing, 2014. 78-79.

[252] Nelson, Bradley, and Ric Thompson. *The Heart of the Emotion Code: Dr. Bradley Nelson on the Effects of Emotional Energy on our Health and Success*. Healthy Wealthy nWise Press, 2014. Kindle Edition. 23, 25, 24, 34.

[253] Ibid.

wounded, or we're feeling deep grief, hurt or loss. It's an assault on the deepest part of our beings."[254]

To compound this assault "what we say to ourselves (through our self-talk) plays a major role in influencing our emotions before and after they have been triggered. If we can only control our self-talk and begin to think and talk more rationally and objectively, we can do a turnabout in our emotions."[255]

We are always vulnerable to misinterpretation in the realm of our ideas and thoughts. To quote Archibald Hart once again: "I am not referring so much to what we see as I am to our thoughts, ideas, and feelings. It is absolutely essential that we realize three important facts about the way we psychologically perceive things:

1. It is not the facts of a situation that determine how we react, but our *perception* of these facts.
2. The way we perceive something may be quite different from what actually happened.
3. We must always give others credit for the way they perceive things and not insist that the only way things are is how we perceive them!"[256]

Which Comes First – Feelings or Thoughts? Realizing what transpires is the finest approach to grasp what takes place and how thoughts and feelings are a two-way street. Emotions have complexities, essentially two levels of emotion have been identified: coarse

---

[254] Ibid.
[255] Ibid.
[256] Nelson, Bradley, and Ric Thompson. *The Heart of the Emotion Code: Dr. Bradley Nelson on the Effects of Emotional Energy on our Health and Success*. Healthy Wealthy nWise Press, 2014. Kindle Edition. 38, 40

and fine. "At the **first** level we have the 'coarse' or fundamental type of emotion, of which there are four: 1) grief; 2) fear; 3) rage; and 4) love. The **second** is a 'fine' or subtle level of emotion which is derived from a combination of these four fundamental types."[257]

Feelings vs. Emotions. Renewing the mind towards kingdom emotions is a requirement to live effectively in a world riddled with negative emotions and feelings. "Intense compassion is the switch that turns on God's healing power,"[258] a switch that allows freedom to be accessible.

"*Feelings* are basically a part of emotion. They are the part of emotion that breaks through into our awareness. A feeling is the sensation or bodily state that accompanies the experience of the emotion. If we are not attending to our emotion, we may not *feel* anything, but the emotion is still there. On the other hand, *emotion* refers to the deeper, underlying state that stirs or agitates us, whether or not we are aware of it as feeling. The term *emotion*, therefore, refers to the state of our being. *Feeling* is how we experience that state. For practical purposes we might as well use both terms interchangeably."[259] People feel what they think. Their emotions are the complete sum of all their thoughts.

The most important understanding you can gain from this is that your ability to succeed in this life will be interfered with by trapped emotions, especially by the heart wall. "You have a unique song to sing. There is a unique creation in your heart. There's a good possibility that it's been locked up inside of you. So many amazing things happen when the heart wall is removed. When the heart wall is taken away, the energy of who you are radiates out and fills

---

[257] Ibid.

[258] Tolman, Kay. *Moved with Compassion: A New Wineskin for Healing and Deliverance.* 2017. 6.

[259] Hart, Archibald D. *Unlocking the Mystery of Your Emotions.* W Publishing Group, 1989. 14.

the universe. People will be drawn to the specific energy you're putting out. The heart wall has been called the greatest discovery in the history of energetic medicine. There is a God above who loves every one of us. He wants us to be free of our emotional baggage so we can find joy in this life."[260] Dr. Nelson has also written: "I believe we're living in the age of the heart. If we can open enough hearts, it will change this world."[261]

However, we know that "change is difficult, but we risk endless difficulties – and often, tragedies – if we don't change. Change requires self-examination, grace, responsibility, humility, discipline, and obedience. Character qualities that run countercultural."[262] We can attain and frequently fulfill the unmet aims of our life by letting go of emotional baggage and by releasing trapped feelings from ourselves, by changing thoughts, feelings, and emotions. This allows us to further improve our health. Getting rid of emotional baggage is the most crucial thing one can do, as this clashes with life.

Basic characteristics of trapped emotions "can occur at any age; are inherited; can occur from within the womb; can be acquired in childhood."[263] Again, the significance of the early formation of beliefs comes into play. Trapped emotions manifest physically or mentally. "To understand how they affect us physically, you must get your mind around this fact: the body is just a very highly organized energy field. That's what we are."[264]

---

[260] Nelson, Bradley, and Ric Thompson. *The Heart of the Emotion Code: Dr. Bradley Nelson on the Effects of Emotional Energy on our Health and Success*. Healthy Wealthy nWise Press, 2014. Kindle Edition. 28-29.

[261] Ibid.

[262] Idleman, Shane. *Help! I'm Addicted: Overcoming the Cravings that Overcome You*. El Paseo Publications, 2019. Kindle Edition. 33.

[263] Nelson, Bradley, and Ric Thompson. *The Heart of the Emotion Code: Dr. Bradley Nelson on the Effects of Emotional Energy on our Health and Success*. Healthy Wealthy nWise Press, 2014. Kindle Edition. 7, 8.
[264] Ibid.

These energy fields being warped by trapped emotions can "contribute to inflammation, pain, congestion, and many diseases, even cancer. Trapped emotions are consistently found in all imbalances that people suffer from. Every disease has trapped emotions as part of that process,"[265] including addictive behaviors, which has been incorrectly labeled as disease.

One last aspect regarding dealing with trapped emotions is that they are accessed in the subconscious mind. "The reality is that the subconscious mind is an archiving, holographic computer that remembers everything you've done, every face you've seen in a crowd and everything you've eaten, tasted, touch or smelled. All our memories are stored away in our bodies."[266] Hence, these memories must be renewed.

To maximize morality and growth of character, "we must optimize brain function. In addition, clearly stated moral teachings act as a guide for the nervous system to know right and wrong. Some people with lower prefrontal cortex PFC activity need anxiety (consequences such as the idea of hellfire and damnation) in order to follow the straight and narrow, and all of us need connectedness with others in order to learn. In summary, a healthy brain is essential to healthy morality and character development (hardware), and along with proper guidance and modeling (software)."[267]

---

[265] Ibid.

[266] Nelson, Bradley, and Ric Thompson. *The Heart of the Emotion Code: Dr. Bradley Nelson on the Effects of Emotional Energy on our Health and Success.* Healthy Wealthy nWise Press, 2014. Kindle Edition. 13.

[267] Amen, Daniel. *Healing the Hardware of the Soul: Enhance Your Brain to Improve Your Work, Love, and Spiritual Life.* New York: Simon & Schuster, 2008. 103.

NOTES PAGE – INTENTIONALLY LEFT BLANK

Biblical Survey Of Types Of Mind

The following table are the scriptural results of scouring the Bible for an understanding of the various references to the mind that must be renewed:

Type of Mind:	Scripture:	Observation:
Right Mind	"And they came to Jesus and looked intently and searchingly at the man who had been a demoniac, sitting there, **clothed and in his right mind,** [the same man] who had had the legion [of demons]; and they were seized with alarm and struck with fear (Mark 5:15 AMPC)."	This man received restored identity which is the evidence of a right mind.
Sober Mind	"But he must be hospitable (loving and a friend to believers, especially to strangers and foreigners); [he must be] a lover of goodness [of good people and good things], **sober-minded** (sensible, discreet), upright and **fair-minded**, a devout man and religiously correct, temperate and keeping himself in hand (Titus 1:8 AMPC)."	The sober mind will cause the leader to be fair in his dealings with God's people.
Spiritual Mind	"For to be carnally minded is death, but to be **spiritually minded** is life and peace (Romans 8:6 NKJV)."	The Spiritual mind is the place of identity. One must consciously choose to receive from the mind of Christ.

Type of Mind:	Scripture:	Observation:
Sound Mind	"For God has not given us a spirit of fear, but of power and of love and of a **sound mind** (2 Timothy 1:7 NKJV)."	<ul><li>I remember Dad Hagin saying that "your spirit knows things your head doesn't know." To add on, if you don't have a sound mind, how can God get through to your spirit?</li><li>Situations may occur that bring opportunities for fear. We may go through some fearful things. But God wants us to endure those moments, suffer them as good soldiers of Jesus Christ and not allow them to define us, but allow them to refine us so that those moments do not become mindsets.</li></ul>
Carnal Mind	"Now the **mind of the flesh** <*carnal*> [which is sense and reason without the Holy Spirit] is death [death that comprises all the miseries arising from sin, both here and hereafter]. But the mind of the [Holy] Spirit is life and [soul] peace [both now and forever] (Romans 8:6 AMPC, emphasis added)."	The spiritual mind is tapping into the mind of the Holy Spirit, which is speaking to your spirit when you understand your identity; that you are created in His image. Through accepting Jesus Christ, you have access to Holy Spirit, and He brings light and soul peace.
Anxious Mind	"And you, do not seek [by meditating and reasoning to inquire into] what you are to eat and what you are to drink; nor be of **anxious** (troubled) **mind** [unsettled, excited, worried, and in suspense] (Luke 12:29 AMPC)."	The anxiety of mind causes one to be troubled and unsettled in all their affairs.
Debased Mind	"And even as they did not like to retain God in their knowledge, God gave them over to a **debased mind**, to do those things which are not fitting (Romans 1:28 NKJV)."	The Amplified bible refers to it as a condemned mind. But there is therefore now no condemnation to those who are in Christ Jesus. Especially when one yokes up with Him as in Matthew 11:28-30.

When one looks at the Romans 12:1-2 renewal, as in the Message Bible, one receives God's help, the help of the Holy Spirit to renew your mind so that you don't reject the truth. We need to be aware of what we are thinking. We should be thinking with a sound, sober, right, spiritual mind. Not with an anxious, carnal, debased mind.

CHAPTER EIGHT: Truth

The Spirit of Truth – Holy Spirit

Believers should allow the Spirit of Truth to reveal where their mind is in an unhealthy rut, such as blaming others for their feelings. If you are allowing someone else to control your feelings and emotions, you are out of control and your responses will be out of control. One must determine to live a spirit-controlled life because the Spirit of Truth will reveal the truth of the matter in love.

In the same way we receive the *baptism of the Holy Spirit*, simply by asking in faith, we can receive the *baptism of love*, which is not found in scripture, see John 13:35. "Similar to other biblical forms of baptisms an immersion in the Father's love deeply changes a person." [268]

Negative behavior transformation and eradication call for "both a behavioral change and a mindset change, oftentimes requiring years of therapy, or in some cases, for those who believe in God, simply an encounter with Holy Spirit."[269] The Ministry of the Holy Spirit can be clearly seen in the following scriptures:

- "But the Comforter (Counselor, Helper, Intercessor, Advocate, Strengthener, Standby), the Holy Spirit, Whom the Father will send in My

---

[268] Tolman, Kay. *Moved with Compassion: A New Wineskin for Healing and Deliverance.* 2017. 22.

[269] Rogers, Gayle. *The Whole Soul: Rescripting Your Life for Personal Transformation.* Kingdom House Publishing, 2014. 109.

name [in My place, to represent Me and act on My behalf], He will teach you all things. And He will cause you to recall (will remind you of, bring to your remembrance) everything I have told you. (John 14:26 AMPC)."

- "And when He comes, He will convict and convince the world and bring demonstration to it about sin and about righteousness (uprightness of heart and right standing with God) and about judgment (John 16:8 AMPC)."

- "But when He, the Spirit of Truth (the Truth-giving Spirit) comes, He will guide you into all the Truth (the whole, full Truth). For He will not speak His own message [on His own authority]; but He will tell whatever He hears [from the Father; He will give the message that has been given to Him], and He will announce and declare to you the things that are to come [that will happen in the future] (John 16:13 AMPC)."

Jesus says that it is the Holy Spirit Who convicts and convinces of sin and of righteousness, which is the goal in seeking first the kingdom. The aspects detailed in these texts above regarding the role of the Holy Spirit provide major areas of assistance for those who are in recovery from abuse. Such people must come out of denial and face the truth. They must cooperate with the Holy Spirit; His role is powerful, and they should not fight against Him. "You must become a partner with God in this reprogramming and renewal process. Such work is a continuous process, not a crisis."[270]

---

[270] Seamands, David A. *Healing for Damaged Emotions*. Wheaton: David C Cook, 1991. 74.

Yes, this Renewal Of The Mind involves our part, and the help of the Holy Spirit. "What is our part in the healing of our damaged emotions? The Holy Spirit is, indeed, the divine counselor, the divine psychiatrist, who gets ahold of our problem on the other end. But we're on this end of it. Just what are you and I supposed to do in this healing process?"[271] As believers, we are to allow the Holy Spirit to dwell within, as in Galatians 5:22, and produce the fruit of His presence, of which the first evidence is love. Love can only blossom when passion is under control. When one's passion is for anything else other than God, is where distortions and addictions can be formed because the passion becomes the quest.

For example, the passion for religion, cocaine, food, people-pleasing, etc. are placed above loving God; the passion is put in the wrong place. Even with overeating, or improper diet; this is why it is called "comfort food" because it is supposed to bring you comfort, which is the role of the Holy Spirit, not the food we eat.

There is a supernatural enabling power given to us through the Holy Spirit that helps us to navigate our natural inclination to run toward the things that are familiar. "Often those who were raised in dysfunctional homes create a dysfunctional atmosphere in their own homes."[272] *Hurting People Hurt People!* The Holy Spirit revealed to me that dysfunction is not an option or an excuse. If not dealt with, dysfunction can be perpetuated to the next generation even though they do not experience direct abuse, their parents pass on the dysfunctional traits.

---

[271] Seamands, David A. *Healing for Damaged Emotions*. Wheaton: David C Cook, 1991. 20.

[272] Meyer, Joyce. *Beauty for Ashes: Receiving Emotional Healing*. Fenton: FaithWords, 2003. 138.

Believers should be guided and influenced namely by the Person of the Holy Spirit which should serve as guide. "What we watch and listen to affects the heart; it's impossible to separate the two. If you truly want to overcome strongholds, you'll need to reprogram your mind."[273]

Gayle Rogers discusses a Hebrew term for Holy Spirt and the breath of God: Ruach. "This same word Ruach, through further etymological study, indicates that this breath imparts "warlike executive and administrative power and energy to men," and is the "mind, seat of emotion, or mental acts, and moral character."[274] This definition demonstrates the connection to the brain's executive functioning which will be discussed in later chapters.

Yet another term for the breath of God, or Holy Spirit, is Pneuma, as in Acts 4:31. "This word Pneuma is a movement of air, a gentle blast, the power by which the human being feels, thinks, and decides. These descriptions indicate that the same Spirit vibrating over the surface of the deep and imparting a vibrating energy, flowing, moving, billowing, and waving motion, impart that same spirit to those who receive the impartation through the power of the indwelling Holy Spirit."[275]

A great biblical example of the role of the Holy Spirit can be seen in the story of Esther and Mordecai. Robert Stearns so eloquently describes this allegory as: "Mordecai, I believe is a picture of the Holy Spirit, the Inner Witness and Guide and Comforter of our hearts. He is a

---

[273] Idleman, Shane. *Help! I'm Addicted: Overcoming the Cravings that Overcome You*. El Paseo Publications, 2019. Kindle Edition. 53.

[274] Rogers, Gayle. *The Whole Soul: Rescripting Your Life for Personal Transformation*. Kingdom House Publishing, 2014. 27.

[275] Ibid.

Father to the Fatherless and the Wonderful Counselor – the one who sticks closer than a brother.

Each of us, when we turn to God, can experience the awakening sound of His voice, His guidance in our hearts. In a very real way, Mordecai became the voice of the Holy Spirit to Esther, hovering and watching over her from her youngest days until now when he is desperately trying to get a word to her in the palace, and ironically having a hard time getting through. How easy it is to rely on the Holy Spirit when we are painfully aware of our lack and our need. How quickly we run to Him for solace, hope, and enrichment. But how quickly His tender voice is lost in the fray once His counsel leads us to the land of blessing. This is the test that Esther faces, and this is the test we face. Can we still hear Mordecai's voice through the thick palace walls of success (page 81, Mordecai)?"[276] Can we still hear the Holy Spirit leading us in the Renewal of the Mind process to live in the truth?

Lies And Deception

Renewal Of The Mind is mandatory to remove the lies that have been implanted. It is the truth that will set you free, and this thesis will expose areas where truth needs to be applied for freedom from addictions which is crucial because lies are like a virus in our soul that when triggered cause contamination. "The things you don't deal with, you cannot heal from. If you

---

[276] Stearns, Robert. *The Cry of Mordecai: Awakening an Esther Generation in a Haman Age*. Shippensburg: Destiny Image Pub, 2009. 81.

don't deal, you cannot heal."[277] True freedom is found in taking responsibility, removing excuses, and asking God for help.

The Apostle Paul asks a probing question in Romans 7:24 that all must encounter *"Who will free me from the domination of sin in my life?'* The answer was given in the previous chapter, Romans 6:16 which says: *Whatever you choose to obey becomes your master*. It all comes down to a person's choice: We can choose sin, or we can choose to obey God. Again, the Holy Spirit is the Helper, not the Chooser. He will help you by revealing the lies, but you must choose to fall out of agreement with these lies to experience authentic freedom.

The biblical allegory of this principle is seen in Genesis 27:41-43. "Jacob has been living on the slippery slope of deceit, and without authenticity, transparency, and integrity – the big three – it was impossible to live a life that honored God."[278] These three elements: authenticity, transparency, and integrity are essential to exposing lies and living in the truth that sets or makes one free. "We don't change truth – truth changes us."[279] However, we must choose truth to experience change!

---

[277] Anderson, Neil T. *Winning the Battle Within: Realistic Steps to Overcoming Sexual Strongholds*. Eugene, OR: Harvest House Pub, 2008. 81.

[278] Gray, John. *Win from Within: Finding Yourself by Facing Yourself*. FaithWords, 2018. 78.

[279] Idleman, Shane. *Help! I'm Addicted: Overcoming the Cravings that Overcome You*. El Paseo Publications, 2019. Kindle Edition. 54.

CHAPTER NINE: Mind vs. Brain

Science of the Brain

To be healthy and happy, the brain and soul require one another. "Understanding the brain-soul connection is the first step in becoming your best self. Optimizing the brain is the next important step to healing the hardware of the soul. To do this, you need to understand your brain's vulnerabilities and develop strategies to overcome them."[280] Gayle Rogers stated that: "I have come to believe that changing the way one thinks is not just a mindset adjustment but can also be correlated in many instances to the way the brain is wired and affected by certain addictive lifestyles."[281]

This concept is discussed in detail by the HeartMath Institute. "In 1991, an organization named the Institute of HeartMath was formed for the specific purpose of exploring the power that human feelings have over the body, and the role that those emotions may play in our world. Specifically, HeartMath chose to focus its research on the place in our bodies where emotion and feeling seem to originate: the human heart."[282]

Modern science is proving this point of the connection of the brain and emotions, they have "discovered that through each emotion we experience in our bodies, we also undergo chemical changes of things such as pH and hormones that mirror our feelings. Through the

---

[280] Amen, Daniel. *Healing the Hardware of the Soul: Enhance Your Brain to Improve Your Work, Love, and Spiritual Life*. New York: Simon & Schuster, 2008. 129.
[281] Rogers, Gayle. *The Whole Soul: Rescripting Your Life for Personal Transformation*. Kingdom House Publishing, 2014. 98.
[282] Braden, Gregg. *The Divine Matrix: Bridging Time, Space, Miracles, and Belief*. Carlsbad: Hay House, 2007. 50.

'positive' experiences of love, compassion, and forgiveness and the 'negative' emotions of hate, judgment, and jealousy, we each possess the power to affirm or deny our existence at each moment of every day. Additionally, the same emotion that gives us such power *within* our bodies extends this force into the quantum world *beyond* our bodies."[283]

This concept assists with the Renewal Of The Mind and addictions. We must renew our mind that we are not a prisoner to the past. We must open our mind to the trap door. "As we have seen, the brain is involved in everything we do: how we think, how we feel, how we act, how we get along with others, how we negotiate, how we pay attention at meetings."[284] Greg Braden adds that "since the space around us is anything but empty. Regardless of what we call it or how science and religion define it, it's clear that there's a field or presence that is the 'great net' that connects everything in creation and links us to the higher power of a greater world."[285]

There is truly a connection between the brain and the Renewal Of The Mind; compassion is at the core. "Whether it is brain chemistry or the prompting of the Holy Spirit, compassion is like a catalyst that motivates us to love and extend God's tender mercy."[286]

---

[283] Braden, Gregg. *The Divine Matrix: Bridging Time, Space, Miracles, and Belief*. Carlsbad: Hay House, 2007. xvii.
[284] Amen, Daniel. *Healing the Hardware of the Soul: Enhance Your Brain to Improve Your Work, Love, and Spiritual Life*. New York: Simon & Schuster, 2008. 124.

[285] Braden, Gregg. *The Divine Matrix: Bridging Time, Space, Miracles, and Belief*. Carlsbad: Hay House, 2007. 28.
[286] Tolman Kay. *Moved with Compassion: A New Wineskin for Healing and Deliverance*. 2017. 16.

Communication – Perception

Perception is a key point to observe regarding communication. Gayle Rogers' view is: "communication is difficult enough without adding malfunctioning mechanisms (i.e., stress, fear, anxiety, toxins, etc.) that would hinder our communication channels even further. And yet, we think we understand and know people well. Sensory integration is described by Wikipedia as 'the neurological process that organizes sensation from one's own body and the environment, thus making it possible to use the body effectively within the environment. Specifically, it deals with how the brain processes multiple sensory modality inputs into usable functional outputs.' Based on these descriptions, it appears that sensory integration encompasses all activity performed during the communication process and is essential for us to comprehend our surroundings."[287]

Daniel Amen was noted to say: "I have frequently spoke at churches about the brain's connection to our daily lives and how behavior becomes problematic when the brain's functioning goes awry. If we are all sinners (very true in my experience of others and myself), and sin, as we have seen, can be related to brain problems, then forgiveness and treatment may go hand in hand. Healing the brain is an important first step in helping people heal their relationship with God."[288] Hence, perception in the healing process is an element of Renewal Of The Mind.

---

[287] Rogers, Gayle. *The Whole Soul: Rescripting Your Life for Personal Transformation*. Kingdom House Publishing, 2014. 143.

[288] Amen, Daniel. *Healing the Hardware of the Soul: Enhance Your Brain to Improve Your Work, Love, and Spiritual Life*. New York: Simon & Schuster, 2008. 105.

Healing is a process that includes many elements, yet "if you still react from an old toxic addictive behavior system which literally has controlled your internal nerve center, you may respond in an entirely different manner. What you should be aware of here is that either there is something in you that needs to be dealt with or something in the other person."[289]

---

[289] Rogers, Gayle. *The Whole Soul: Rescripting Your Life for Personal Transformation*. Kingdom House Publishing, 2014. 106.

CHAPTER TEN: Transformation

Using both behavioral change and cognitive behavior modalities, believers can take their lives back after years of dysfunctionality. "When you can get a person to see and acknowledge their own negative patterns, they are well on their way to recovery."[290]

Shame is the source of many complex inner problems, such as:

- "Alienation; Depression; Failure syndrome; Isolating loneliness; Lack of confidence; Perfectionism; Timidity (fear of all types); Deep sense of inferiority; Neurotic behavior; Compulsive behavior.
- Inability to develop and maintain healthy relationships."[291]

Additionally, shame "pulls down the whole level of one's personality, and results in a vulnerability to the other negative emotions, and therefore, often produces false pride, anger, and guilt."[292]

---

[290] Rogers, Gayle. *The Whole Soul: Rescripting Your Life for Personal Transformation*. Kingdom House Publishing, 2014. 112.

[291] Meyer, Joyce. *Beauty for Ashes: Receiving Emotional Healing*. Fenton: FaithWords, 2003. 93.

[292] Hawkins, David R. *Power vs. Force: The Hidden Determinants of Human Behavior*. Carlsbad: Hay House, 2013. Kindle Edition. 80.

Guidelines for Transformation:

1) "You will need to be aligned properly with people who support you in your efforts to change.

2) You must be passionate about what you are doing and where you are right now despite all opposition and circumstances.

3) You must be celebrated among your peers or sphere of influence and not just tolerated.

4) Your focus must always be on helping others less fortunate than yourself, lest you remain in your own self-centeredness.

5) You must be ever increasing in wisdom, love, understanding, and revelation.

6) You must have the courage to never stop; become an unstoppable force with singleness of purpose.

7) You should always be developing and training a team of warriors with like minds with the ability to duplicate the model you have fashioned.

8) You must be willing to maintain a lifestyle of a transformed mind with daily training and control your thoughts to line up with your purpose.

9) You must know how to walk on top of your circumstances, chaos, and confusion and not get under them.

10) Understand that your assignment on earth is not about you and your gift, but rather fulfilling the advancement of the Kingdom."[293]

---

[293] Rogers, Gayle. *The Whole Soul: Rescripting Your Life for Personal Transformation*. Kingdom House Publishing, 2014. 154-162.

PART TWO: DICHOTOMY OF ADDICTIONS

CHAPTER ELEVEN: Possible Causes of Addictions

There are verified roots of addiction. The following is a brief list of entry points of addiction:

- Trauma
- PTSD
- People pleasing, or performance orientation
- Grief
- Self-medicating verses trusting the triune God
- The Screwtape Element according Malachi chapter four, father's role out of alignment
- Fragmented soul
- Core issues located below the surface, or subconscious
- Passivity of the mind, will, and emotions
- An orphan spirit can cause people to manifest addictions

Additionally, persons may possess an addictive personality which "can include addictions to drug and alcohol abuse, pornography, gambling, internet, videogames, food, exercise, work and even relationships with others. It is further described as the: excessive, repetitive use of pleasurable activities to cope with unmanageable internal conflict, pressure, and stress."[294]

Another root is boredom and depression. "The more boredom becomes a problem, the more prone we are to seek ways of escape through drugs and alcohol (which are the most common forms of self-treatment for depression). Whatever our station in life and regardless of our age or sex, none of us can claim to be totally free of depression."[295] Not only depression, but "many problems are due to lifestyle choices, and therefore, we need to start there. Reaching for a pill as soon as we feel anxious is rarely the best solution."[296] Many people are addicted to years of emotional issues which lead to toxic stress that results in addictive behaviors.

Adverse Childhood Experiences (ACEs) are another contributing factor to addictive behaviors. People with high ACE scores who experienced the cumulative effect of growing up with a cluster of adverse childhood experiences tended to be those who fell into the healthcare and penal systems in adulthood because studies suggest their childhood stress was more than their brain/body could process. "Life is an *ongoing* battle. When we are on God's side, we are also on the enemy's hit list. Resistance tests our faith, draws us closer to God, and can lead to spiritual maturity."[297]

---

[294] Rogers, Gayle. *The Whole Soul: Rescripting Your Life for Personal Transformation*. Kingdom House Publishing, 2014. 99.

[295] Hart, Archibald D. *Unlocking the Mystery of Your Emotions*. W Publishing Group, 1989. 75.
[296] Idleman, Shane. *Help! I'm Addicted: Overcoming the Cravings that Overcome You*. El Paseo Publications, 2019. Kindle Edition. 67, 17.

[297] Ibid.

Demonic Influence

The trust of the innocent is the liar's most useful tool. This saying exposes how the enemy preys on unknowing victims. This type of demonic influence is a major contributing factor to addictions. One author "believes the kingdom of darkness is still present and Satan is intent on making the lives of Christians miserable, keeping us from enjoying and exercising our inheritance in Christ. Our only option in the conflict is how and to what extent we are going to wage the battle. This author noted that if we fail to perceive our access to Christ's authority in our lives; therefore, we will live in bondage."[298] See Ephesians 1:22 and 26 for a further view of the authority that believers are to possess.

The Passion Translation summarizes this influence: "Who has anguish? Who has bitter sorrow? Who constantly complains and argues? Who stumbles and falls and hurts himself? Who's the one with bloodshot eyes? It's the one who drinks too much and is always looking for a brew. Make sure it's never you! And don't be drunk with wine but be known as one who enjoys the company of the lovers of God, for drunkenness brings the sting of a serpent, like the fangs of a viper spreading poison into your soul. It will make you hallucinate, mumble, and speak words that are perverse (Proverbs 23:29-33 TPT)."

Verse 32 of this Proverb is comparable with Ephesians 5:18, where the Apostle Paul admonishes believers to not be drunk with wine, but to be drunk with Holy Spirit. It is worldly drunkenness that is poisoning the soul to the point to where the mind is not strong enough to

---

[298] Rogers, Gayle. *Healing The Traumatized Soul*. AuthorHouse, 2005. 103.

receive the mind of Christ. This sting of a serpent is symbolic of the poison of demonic power that can cause addictions and rule over the soul. One version refers to the sting as *an adder*. The enemy is releasing adder eggs at an early age, that when a person grows up, these eggs become activated and *bite* according to Isaiah 59:5.

The two voices that we hear contrasted all throughout the book of Proverbs is the voice of wisdom & the voice of a harlot (religion). Additionally, these two voices can be viewed as creation & conscience which, continually speak to our hearts. Brilliance of intellect is not required, only an attentive and tender heart. This type of wisdom comes from being led by the Holy Spirit. Here is an example of this concept: "Can't you hear the voice of Wisdom? From the top of the mountains of influence she speaks into the gateways of the glorious city. At the place where pathways merge, at the entrance of every portal, there she stands, ready to impart understanding, shouting aloud to all who enter, preaching her sermon to those who will listen (Proverbs 8:1-3 TPT)."

Another aspect of exposing demonic influences is recognizing the problematic spiritual high places of idolatry as discussed in the following list of scriptures: 1 Kings 15:14; 22:43; 2 Kings 12:3; 14:4; 15:4; 15:35. Derek Prince says: "Christians must learn to think if they are to defeat Satan. And you are going to need your mind to fully grasp the importance of this topic of removing the high places."[299]

High places proved to be a source of continual conflict with the children of Israel. "The Israelites constantly struggled between obeying God by worshipping Him in the appointed place and disobeying Him by going back to the high places."[300] Yet the rightful

---

[299] Rogers, Gayle. *Healing The Traumatized Soul*. AuthorHouse, 2005. 103.
[300] Prince, Derek. *Pulling Down Strongholds*. Charlotte: Whitaker House, 2013. 69.

place of worship is the place where God's name abides according to Deuteronomy 12:5, 11, and 21.

Passiveness or Aggressiveness

When finally deciding to no longer be passive aggressive, but assertive, one must deal with the root issues that caused the passive aggressive behavior. By doing so, one will gain the capacity to be Christlike assertive, He knew when to assert passivity or aggression. This must be learned through a spirit-controlled temperament as in Psalm 139:23-24, in the searching of the heart, God can reveal areas that need assertiveness, and anything within the heart that is blocking the capacity to be assertive. He will expose things within the heart to be dealt with by the help of the Holy Spirit. "Do not be passive and expect victory to just fall on you. It does come by the grace of God, and not by our works, but we must actively cooperate with the Holy Spirit each step of the way."[301]

A fundamental principle is that individuals are response-able. They are *ABLE* to be accountable for their responses to life's triggers. "The assertive Christian is *able* to respond in various ways to people and events. The assertive Christian makes choices."[302] These

---

[301] Meyer, Joyce. *Beauty for Ashes: Receiving Emotional Healing*. Fenton: FaithWords, 2003. 208.
[302] Koch, Ruth N., and Kenneth C. Haugk. *Speaking the Truth in Love: How to be an Assertive Christian*. St Louis: Stephen Ministries St Louis, 1992. 31.

choices display outward signs of an integrated personality and the understanding of assertive skills.

"When you possess assertion skills, you are *able* to make a deliberate choice about whether to behave assertively, passively, or aggressively. Knowing how to behave assertively allows you to be intentional about your own behavior rather than having the situation dictate how you'll behave. You can be proactive rather than reactive."[303]

Addictive behavior robs assertion skills because one thinks that aggressiveness or passiveness is the way, instead of assertiveness. The goal is to learn assertion skills so that one will know when it is time to be either or. The Screwtape Element is to skew people's mind (which is the battlefield) to always being aggressive, or only homing in on the aggressive things that Jesus did in scripture, or vice versa, never realizing that Jesus's passive and aggressive behaviors were controlled by assertive skills.

Believers will also need the whole counsel of God, and not be found taking things out of context. As well as establishing things with two to three witnesses. People may become addictive because they do not know how to be assertive. Instead of being assertive, they self-medicate. "Assertive behavior is behavior that honors the self while honoring others. The assertive person authentically cares for others and at the same time engages in God-pleasing self-care."[304]

According to 2 Timothy 1:7 TEV, being timid is being passive. Yet having a sound mind brings self-control. Believers must renew the mind to not act out of a fear response when

---

[303] Koch, Ruth N., and Kenneth C. Haugk. *Speaking the Truth in Love: How to be an Assertive Christian*. St Louis: Stephen Ministries St Louis, 1992. 175, 23.
[304] Ibid.

things happen to make one timid or fearful. But to renew the mind with the help of the Holy Spirit which produces self-control and the fruit of a sound mind that has been renewed with the word.

Attitudes of passivity are not pleasing to God. It is the assertive lifestyle which merges the faith life, thinking patterns, and behavior choices to be in alignment with the mind of Christ. "Assertive thinking seeks the truth by challenging irrational beliefs and by trying to determine what is unreasonable, illogical, or absurd, and then rejecting those thoughts."[305]

See the temptation of Jesus in Luke 4:1-13, far too large a quote to include. However, "notice that in each case Jesus responded to the temptation as if He had a choice. And because Jesus had a clear sense of His identity as a person who belonged to God, His sense of personal connection to God shaped and empowered His choices in the face of temptation. Jesus dealt with each temptation by asserting His personal identity."[306] What a notable example for believers learning identity in Christ!

Unresolved Anger

Anger alone is not harmful, assuming it does not escalate into angry behavior, but is resolved swiftly. "Undealt with, it has the potential for being transformed into hostility and

---

[305] Koch, Ruth N., and Kenneth C. Haugk. *Speaking the Truth in Love: How to be an Assertive Christian.* St Louis: Stephen Ministries St Louis, 1992. 33, 58.
[306] Ibid.

hence becomes sin."[307] Many have experienced feelings of anger but are not sure how to define anger. "One unabridged dictionary defines it as 'a strong feeling of displeasure excited by a real or supposed injury; often accompanied by a desire to take vengeance or to obtain satisfaction from the offending party. The key words in this definition are *strong feeling, injury,* and *vengeance.* Anger always has these three components, and we will see that the key to dealing with anger lies in dealing with these components."[308]

Frankly, feelings of anger "are important signals of a violation, but these feelings should be heeded and disposed of quickly."[309] Anger is also connected to depression. "The most concise definition of depression I know is this: 'Depression is frozen rage.' If you have a consistently genuine problem with depression, you have not resolved some area of anger in your life. [310] Oftentimes, "the roots of depression are buried in the subsoil of early family life. And unless you learn to deal honestly with those angry roots, to face your resentment and forgive, you'll be living in a greenhouse where depression is sure to flourish."[311] The aftereffects of anger and unforgiveness can cause hatred, wrath, and strife, which are listed as works of the flesh in Galatians 5:19-20.

Anger can be either expressed, or the other option is for anger to implode. "Some anger explodes inward, resulting in depression, a tendency toward addictions, suicidal thoughts, or

---

[307] Hart, Archibald D. *Unlocking the Mystery of Your Emotions*. W Publishing Group, 1989. 73, 44.

[308] Ibid.
[309] Ibid. 72.

[310] Seamands, David A. *Healing for Damaged Emotions*. Wheaton: David C Cook, 1991. 125.

[311] Ibid.

even suicide. What people hide and deny will dominate them."[312] These life issues must be addressed, and the perspective renewed beyond the hurt. "Life is full of potential for hurt and thus can create anger at every turn. It is inevitable that we will be hurt by *people* and by *circumstances.* People hurt us *because* they are human. They make mistakes; they are selfish and self-centered; they demand perfection and are intolerant of our mistakes. In fact, they are just as human as we are!"[313]

Anger is not to become a lifestyle – unless one seeks self-destruction. Anger itself cannot be stored up. However, the trapped trauma in one's body from ACEs, or even from traumatic experiences in our adulthood, if these are not properly processed, they may operate as poison within the physical body. Emotions are not visibly seen, however the effects of the chemical changes within the body are being seen in chronic illnesses. There are physical connections to what is happening within the body. Be mindful to expose this with love, and to extend compassion to those who are trapped in negative feelings and lead them in proper ways to operate assertive instead of passive aggressive.

"To be correct, what we do 'store' are the memories of hurts, the resentments, that have the ability to *recreate* anger in us in the present."[314] This is why Renewal Of The Mind is crucial so that when the memory of the hurt arises, one is not triggered to anger. "Forgiveness holds the most promise for aiding us to effectively resolve our feelings of anger."[315]

---

[312] Koch, Ruth N., and Kenneth C. Haugk. *Speaking the Truth in Love: How to be an Assertive Christian*. St Louis: Stephen Ministries St Louis, 1992. 144-145.
[313] Hart, Archibald D. *Unlocking the Mystery of Your Emotions*. W Publishing Group, 1989. 68, 71, 58, 72.
[314] Ibid.
[315] Ibid.

Trauma – ACEs

Trauma due to adverse childhood experiences (ACEs) is a major factor in addictions. "Studies report that Black women who experienced childhood sexual abuse, domestic violence, and sexual assault consistently had higher rates of substance and alcohol abuse than their peers, including marijuana and crack cocaine."[316] These statistics are not limited to the African American community, but to all races. Trauma and ACEs are anti-discriminatory. There is a postulation that "four trauma-causing factors or traumagenic dynamics are: 1) traumatic sexualization, 2) betrayal, 3) powerlessness and 4) stigmatization. These dynamics alter children's cognitive and emotional orientation to the world and create trauma by distorting children's self-concept, worldview, and affective capacities."[317]

The faith community must do better at addressing these types of root causes. "Rather than listen and respond to the narratives of their hurting women, black churches have put their time and energy into programs varying from national usher's day, revivals, crusades and conventions, to pastor's appreciations, women's missions, and annual picnics. There has been no time left to address the bombarding issues abused women face on a day-to-day basis."[318] Truly a modern day Screwtape Element against womanhood. The faith community must learn

---

[316] Rogers, Gayle. *Healing The Traumatized Soul*. AuthorHouse, 2005. 29, 61, 77.
[317] Ibid.

[318] Ibid.

to listen and love. "Listening can be the best medicine. To have ears that really hear you must be emotionally present with no agenda."[319]

Tana Amen shared portions of her testimony and the *seedlings* for trauma as follows: "My fury raged internally at my mother for thinking I should be polite to a predator, and that black seed of anger turned into a dark root of resentment that I wouldn't fully recognize for years. When he molested me, he'd violated her trust. She believed she'd failed as a mother, as a protector, and as a woman, and she was having a lot of trouble getting over that."[320] This is an example of how the trauma impacted multi-generations.

Damaged Emotions

In her book *Beauty for Ashes,* Joyce Meyer discusses two types of emotional pain: "1) the pain of change, and 2) the pain of never changing and remaining the same."[321] She goes further to say this about the role of damaged emotions: "My problems were not in my home life or my marriage, but in me, in my wounded, crippled emotions."[322]

---

[319] Tolman, Kay. *Moved with Compassion: A New Wineskin for Healing and Deliverance.* 2017. 41.

[320] Amen, Tana. *The Relentless Courage of a Scared Child: How Persistence, Grit, and Faith Created a Reluctant Healer.* Nashville: Thomas Nelson, 2021. 96.

[321] Meyer, Joyce. *Beauty for Ashes: Receiving Emotional Healing.* Fenton: FaithWords, 2003. 53, 140.

[322] Ibid.

These crippled emotions can be the culprit and "cause generational hatred and may even infect our DNA."[323] In reality, childhood should produce favorable emotions because "someone has said, 'Your childhood is the time of life when God desires to build the rooms of the temple in which He wants to live when you are an adult.' What a beautiful thought! Parents have the privilege, and heavy responsibility, of giving the basic design to the temple – the child's self-image."[324]

Another blatant Screwtape Element is that of low self-esteem, which "is Satan's deadliest psychological weapon, and it can keep you marching around in vicious circles of fear and uselessness."[325] We must renew our mind from a low self-esteem to a healthy identity in Christ, from a low self-esteem to the identity as sons and daughters of God.

"You will never receive healing for your damaged emotions until you stop blaming everyone else and accept your responsibility."[326] Some aspects of our everyday existence require healing by the Holy Spirit. "They are not subject to ordinary prayer, discipline, and willpower, they need a special kind of understanding, an unlearning of past wrong programming, and a relearning and reprogramming transformation by the renewal of our minds. And this is not done overnight by a crisis experience."[327]

Erroneous theology must be corrected. God has made believers to possess proper self-esteem. If one goes against this, they are not only following wrong theology, but flirting with

---

[323] Amen, Daniel. *Healing the Hardware of the Soul: Enhance Your Brain to Improve Your Work, Love, and Spiritual Life*. New York: Simon & Schuster, 2008. 119.
[324] Seamands, David A. *Healing for Damaged Emotions*. Wheaton: David C Cook, 1991. 64.

[325] Ibid. 56, 21, 14, 73.
[326] Ibid.
[327] Ibid.

their own destruction. Believers must "develop the picture of your worth and value from God, not from the false reflections that come out of your past. The healing of low self-esteem really hinges on a choice you must make: Will you listen to Satan as he employs all the lies, the distortions, the put-downs, and the hurts of your past to keep you bound by unhealthy, unchristian feelings and concepts about yourself? Or will you receive your self-esteem from God and His word?"[328] This leads right into the next cause of addictions.

Memory Repression

Memories are a vital part of our makeup. These memories from the past and present must be integrated to a state of healthiness. "The temporal lobes and deep limbic system, which process and help store memories, are also involved in character development. The sum of our memories and experiences is responsible for our sense of identity and connectedness to those around us, as well as our character."[329]

Therefore, Renewal Of The Mind is essential for the memories to be renewed. Yet for them to be renewed, they must be remembered. Hence, understanding the varying types of memories will expose the Screwtape Element to the Renewal Of The Mind process which is to cause disassociation and fragmentation of memories.

---

[328] Ibid.

[329] Amen, Daniel. *Healing the Hardware of the Soul: Enhance Your Brain to Improve Your Work, Love, and Spiritual Life*. New York: Simon & Schuster, 2008. 91.

An important type of memory are repressed memories. "Memory repression is a useful and necessary tool that unburdens your mind, leaving you free to focus your conscious energy on the here and now. The traumatic and the trivial are the two kinds of information your mind represses. Trauma is any shock, wound, or bodily injury that may be either remembered or repressed, depending on your needs, your age, and the nature of the trauma."[330]

Repression of memory often is a result of abuse and trauma. Abuse can be defined as a trauma inflicted deliberately, wrongly, and unjustly to harm another human being. These traumatic events are ideal as memory repression thrives in shame, secrecy, and shock normally induced by such abuse and trauma. Many people who turn to addictive behavior, which have been anesthetizing the painful memories, such as "the addiction of drugs, alcohol, food, gambling, or sex has served to stop the memories from emerging and has medicated the pain caused by the abuse."[331] When sober, the memories emerge and must be healed.

Those haunting memories remain inside a person, recorded, and stored in the filing system in the brain to be accessed at the most inopportune time, or causing addictive behaviors. "Human beings have five kinds of memory. The mind has a process of recording, storing, and retrieving everything that happens by using at least one of these memory processes: 1) Recall, 2) Imagistic, 3) Feeling, 4) Body, and 5) Acting-out memories."[332]

---

[330] Fredrickson, Renee. *Repressed Memories: A Journey to Recovery from Sexual Abuse*. New York: Simon & Schuster, 1992. 22.

[331] Ibid. 37, 88-94.
[332] Ibid.

Conflict Avoidance

Many people choose to avoid conflict at the cost of peace, their own peace, and the peace of others, by not taking responsibility for their own actions. However, problems do not disappear by avoiding them. "So many people have orchestrated their lives to avoid the conflict of facing their true selves in an effort to trick people into thinking that they're something they're actually not. What an exhausting enterprise it must be to live a life hoping to please people with a truth that is not yours. Here's a secret: God is looking for the authentic you, not the projected you. The you He created is the you He can redeem. But He will not redeem what is projected as perfection and what is assumed as autonomous."[333]

Depression

Depression might be caused by psychological triggers, "since our minds and bodies operate in unison the depression recruits glands and hormones to be a part of the experience. The depressive ideas cause our bodies to respond in a depressed way, producing changes in our stomach, respiration, heartbeat, and so on. Together with the thoughts, they constitute the total depression package."[334]

---

[333] Gray, John. *Win from Within: Finding Yourself by Facing Yourself*. FaithWords, 2018. 143.

[334] Hart, Archibald D. *Unlocking the Mystery of Your Emotions*. W Publishing Group, 1989. 77.

This may explain why depression does not disappear when the source of the depression has been eliminated. "Our needs disturb body chemistry, and it takes time for it to restore itself. I am stressing this here because so often we forget to make allowances for our biological involvement in depression. The speed with which our system returns to normal will depend on several factors, including:

- The depth of your depression (the deeper the depression, the longer it will take for your system to recover);

- The nature of your physiology (some of us have systems that require a longer recovery time than others);

- Whether there are distracting factors (if you are recovering from a depression and find yourself taken up with some other engaging activity, you are likely to recover more rapidly than if your activity is not distracting).

- These factors all determine how quickly you will return to normal."[335]

Depression has highly physical manifestations. Yet many people are opposed to taking medication to correct imbalances. "Many severely depressed people avoid appropriate help because they fear becoming hooked on medication. If you have weak eyes, you don't hesitate to wear corrective glasses. If you suffer from diabetes, you take insulin. If you have a biochemical or genetic predisposition toward depression, you should feel just as much freedom in taking the proper treatment. Remember, though, that anti-depressant medications

---

[335] Hart, Archibald D. *Unlocking the Mystery of Your Emotions*. W Publishing Group, 1989. 78, 77.

do nothing for psychological depression."³³⁶ The medication is an aid in dealing with and healing the psychological concerns.

---

³³⁶ Ibid.

Denial

Denial is a defense mechanism that has spread like a cancer throughout nations as well as the Christian Church by individuals and entire congregations. This malignancy is deteriorating the very edifice that should be a place of safety to expose denial which is "the psychological defense mechanism in which confrontation with a personal problem or with reality is avoided by denying the existence of the problem or reality."[337]

The root of much denial is fear. Greg Braden shares the following: "I invite seminar participants to complete a preprinted form asking them to identify the greatest patterns of their childhood caretakers that they would consider 'negative.' I ask for the negative patterns because I've seen people trapped in the positive patterns of joy in their lives. Universally, the situations that cause people to feel stuck have roots in what are considered negative feelings. These are the emotions that we have about our own experiences and what they mean to us in our lives. And while we can't alter *what* has happened, we can understand *why* we feel as we do and change what our life history means to us."[338]

These fears are a great companion or hiding place for denial. "Universal patterns of fear may be so subtle in their expression yet so painful to recall that we skillfully create the masks that make them bearable. Like the way a difficult family memory is always there yet seldom discussed, we have unconsciously agreed to disguise the hurt of our collective past in

---

[337] Stearns, Robert. *The Cry of Mordecai: Awakening an Esther Generation in a Haman Age*. Shippensburg: Destiny Image Pub, 2009. 63.

[338] Braden, Gregg. *The Divine Matrix: Bridging Time, Space, Miracles, and Belief*. Carlsbad: Hay House, 2007. 152.

ways that are socially acceptable. Due to the ways we mask our fear, we never have to talk about the deepest hurts of our lives. Yet they remain with us, lingering and unresolved, until something happens, and we can no longer simply look in another direction. When we allow ourselves to go a little deeper into these powerful, unmasked moments of life, what we discover is that as different as all our fears appear to be, they resolve into one of only three basic patterns (or a combination of the three): the fear of separation and abandonment, the fear of low self-worth, and the fear of surrender and trust."[339]

---

[339] Braden, Gregg. *The Divine Matrix: Bridging Time, Space, Miracles, and Belief*. Carlsbad: Hay House, 2007. 153.

CHAPTER TWELVE: Types of Addictions

The number of addictive behaviors that can manifest into abuse may seem unlimited. Nevertheless, the following is a partial list before we delve deeper into these conditions:

- "Substance abuse: Alcohol; Drugs (illegal and prescription).
- Monetary obsessions: Excessive spending; Hoarding.
- Food disorders: Bulimia (binge-purge); Anorexia (self-starvation); Obesity caused by gluttony.
- Feeling addictions: Rage; Sadness; Fear; Excessive excitement; Religious righteousness; Joy fixation.
- Thought addictions: Excessive detailing; Worry; Nonstop talking; Lustful thoughts; Unsettled mind.
- Activity obsessions: Work; Sports; Reading; Gambling; Exercise; Television viewing; Owning and caring for excessive numbers of pets.
- Will addictions: Controlling; Controlled; Reenactment addicts; Caretaker."[340]

These addictions can lead to guilt and condemnation, which in fact increase sin. The addiction then breeds guilt. Joyce Meyer shared the following regarding the role of guilt:

---

[340] Meyer, Joyce. *Beauty for Ashes: Receiving Emotional Healing.* Fenton: FaithWords, 2003. 32-35, 86.

"Before I learned about God's grace, I can never remember being guilt-free!"[341] These types of guilt feelings rob faith; "if you have lived for a long time buried under a load of guilt and condemnation, your faith may need to be strengthened."[342] The following section will delve deeper into a few of the addictive behaviors mentioned in the list above.

Smoking appears to be harmless, yet it is one of the leading causes of preventable premature disease and death in the United States. All age groups are impacted by smoking. Youth yield to peer pressure. As well, adults are pressured with social smoking. Many think that smoking is harmless, but it is never harmless. Although smoking products are a legal substance, it is highly addictive and a difficult habit to break.

The new phenomenon of Vape and CBD products have added to the plethora of smoking problems. The newfound use of vape pens and devices may be creating unknown problems as studies still aren't clear on the damage to the human body that is being created by these devices. Yet common sense would say there is some type of damage because it is introducing foreign substances into the human body.

Drugs and alcohol are usually the main categories that people think of when they think of addictions. The visibility of intoxication due to drugs and alcohol are easier to recognize than other types of addictions. Distinct types of substances have emerged and are now classed as drugs and alcohol, such as huffing household items, etc.

---

[341] Ibid.
[342] Meyer, Joyce. *Beauty for Ashes: Receiving Emotional Healing*. Fenton: FaithWords, 2003. 88.

Social Media Gaming; Internet Usage has altered our way of life, from how we obtain our news to how we communicate with our loved ones. Like substance usage, social media, gaming, and excessive internet usage can trigger dopamine spikes. Social media is an enticing mix of distraction and reward that can be difficult to resist. Regardless, it is easy to get drawn into very real perils to the quality of productivity, emotions, sleep, relationships, and more. In some dire cases, this cycle traps young individuals in the early phases of identity formation, never allowing them to progress toward self-actualization and maturity.

Additionally, "the observed and documented negative health and psychosocial consequences include a range of health conditions that share signs and symptoms with disorders such as gambling disorder and substance use disorders. Consider also what consequences those 'short-term, dopamine-driven feedback loops might have on an individual's mental health and well-being. Here's the point: When looking at the dangers of social media, we must not only consider our natural, biological reward responses, but also the fact that this new digital environment is hazardous *by design*."[343]

The internet can be accessed for even what seems to be good, for example grief online support groups. Whatever is allowed to take center stage in one's life has the capacity to be an addiction, which is idolatry. The American Psychiatric Association's Diagnostic and Statistical Manual of Mental Disorders (DSM) is being updated to include excessive internet use.

---

[343] Jantz, Gregory. *Social Media and Depression: How to Be Healthy and Happy in the Digital Age*. Peabody: Aspire Press, 2021. 21.

It is understood that all social media cannot be completely avoided. "Rather than suggesting that at-risk people simply avoid social media altogether, one recent study concluded that 'individuals with Major Depressive Disorder or depressive symptoms should develop an awareness of the specific negative social media behaviors that may exacerbate their depressive symptoms and acquire an understanding of positive social media behaviors that may reduce those symptoms."[344]

It is apparent that "young people already experience elevated mental and emotional stresses associated with adolescence, helping them navigate the online world safely is paramount. The stakes can literally be a matter of life and death."[345] Truthfully speaking, engagement with digital media influences the human brain similar to other mood-altering substances.

Another connection with this addictive behavior is that of depression and anxiety. "These associations are strong enough that it may be valuable for clinicians to ask individuals with depression and anxiety about multiple platform use and to counsel regarding this potential contributing factor."[346] The greater the likelihood of depression, the more people are prone to use social media as an escape. The more they use social media, the more depressed they become. It is a never-ending cycle.

Toxic content is another adverse dimension of constant internet usage, social media, and gaming. "It should come as no surprise that a steady diet of 'digital distortion' and persistent pessimism endangers mental health and magnifies depression symptoms."[347] There

---

[344] Jantz, Gregory. *Social Media and Depression: How to Be Healthy and Happy in the Digital Age*. Peabody: Aspire Press, 2021. 40, 23, 13, 29, 71.
[345] Ibid.
[346] Ibid.
[347] Ibid.

have been studies performed which detail how emotional states can be manipulated through social media. Continually intaking, or even casually browsing over emotionally charged posts and comments might cause the reader to experience emotional states of change.

The following list details elements of excessive internet and social media use which are in character with that of substance abuse and therefore "justify a substance abuse disorder diagnosis:

Impaired Control	1) Taking more or for longer than intended. 2) Unsuccessful efforts to stop or cut down use. 3) Spending a great deal of time obtaining, using, or recovering from use. 4) Craving for substance.
Social Impairment	5) Failure to fulfill major obligations due to use. 6) Continued use despite problems caused or exacerbated by use. 7) Important activities given up or reduced because of substance use.
Risky Use	8) Recurrent use in hazardous situations. 9) Continued use despite physical or psychological problems that are caused or exacerbated by substance use.
Pharmacologic Dependence	10) Tolerance to effects of the substance. 11) Withdrawal symptoms when not using or using less."[348]

Lastly, validation is an issue with the use of social media, gaming, and the internet; these are unreliable sources of validation. "Self-validation involves the process of allowing yourself to acknowledge your efforts and feelings in a way that makes it unnecessary to seek those things from others."[349] Many are seeking validation and confirmation in these incorrect places.

---

[348] Jantz, Gregory. *Social Media and Depression: How to Be Healthy and Happy in the Digital Age*. Peabody: Aspire Press, 2021. 32-33, 78, 81.
[349] Ibid.

Believers are encouraged to "protect yourself by replacing validation on social media with validation from real life relationships with people who know and care about you, validation from yourself, and validation from God."[350]

Gambling and Shopping. Compulsive gambling and shopping can be an addiction. Many people jokingly refer to compulsive shopping as *retail therapy*. The rush from finding a good deal or sale can be just as intoxicating as a dopamine hit from using a substance. The same can be said of gambling, it is the compulsive thrill chasing that again overloads the dopamine centers in the brain.

Food. If guilt is not dealt with it can cause one to self-medicate. One example is of guilt-eating instead of feeding the body. Comfort foods are generally high in carbohydrates and sugar, which can cause a drain in the body instead of the perceived comfort. The combination of guilt and sin are buttons that can 'push' a person into addictive behavior. Guilt is an addiction itself. As stated in the list above regarding food disorders, bulimia, anorexia, and obesity all have a mental or emotional root cause.

Sexual addiction is coming to the forefront in the Christian community more rampantly. Steve Gallagher, in his book *Counseling the Sexual Addict* doesn't label it an "*addiction* to indicate a disease or to lesson personal responsibility for one's behavior; rather,

---
[350] Ibid.

it is shorthand for life-dominating sexual sins that can be conquered through the Word of God and intense discipleship."[351]

June Hunt discusses three types of sexual addiction as: "compulsive, immoral, and enslaving."[352] Sexual desire is normal; however, lust is the element that drives most sexual addictions. Another fuel to sexual addictions is pornography, which many view as harmless. Yet pornography can be related as a quicksand to sexual addictions.

At the core of every sexual addict "is a sense of shame – because they feel unlovable, unworthy, and unwanted – shame resulting from repeated failure and abandonment."[353] June Hunt created an acronym from the word SHAME based on the scripture found in Proverbs 18:3:

"**S** – Secretive

H – Hollow

A – Abusive

M – Mood-altering

E – Essential."[354]

Along with shame, abandonment is another core of ALL sexual addiction. A few key scriptures to meditate on for freedom from sexual addictions are 1 Corinthians 6:18 and 1 Thessalonians 4:1-8. To walk in freedom, the following three-fold approach is suggested: "acquiring knowledge about genuine, healthy intimacy; committing to sexual behavior only

---

[351] Gallagher, Steve. *A Biblical Guide to Counseling the Sexual Addict*. Dry Ridge: Steve Gallagher, 2005. 8.
[352] Hunt, June. *How to Defeat Harmful Habits: Freedom from Six Addictive Behaviors*. Eugene: Harvest House Publishers, 2011. 288-289.
[353] Ibid. 298, 299.

[354] Ibid.

in marriage; and coming to the understanding that our most important need is not sex but intimacy in a relationship – acceptance, approval, affection."[355] In recent years, sexual addictions in the church have come to the forefront. However, these issues have always been present, just hidden and hushed.

People Pleasing; Perfectionism. What exactly is perfectionism? It can be difficult to define or describe perfectionism, therefore, the following progressive list of symptoms will help to identify the concern: "1) Tyranny of the oughts. 2) Self-depreciation. 3) Anxiety. 4) Legalism. 5) Anger. 6) Denial."[356] This last symptom, denial, is the mixture of legalism and performance and can cause deep emotional problems to set in and is identifying the progression of perfectionism which is a catalyst or hallmark of those who are trapped in addictions.

---

[355] Hunt, June. *How to Defeat Harmful Habits: Freedom from Six Addictive Behaviors*. Eugene: Harvest House Publishers, 2011. 321.

[356] Seamands, David A. *Healing for Damaged Emotions*. Wheaton: David C Cook, 1991. 77-83.

CHAPTER THIRTEEN: The Brain And Addictions

The Brain

The Amen Clinic's business slogan is "Transforming The Way Mental Health Is Treated."[357] They have made historical advances in looking at the brain and addictions. The clinic uses the following foundational points, which are powerful for Renewal Of The Mind. They are called "the four circles:

1) Biology (genetics, head injuries, diseases, etc.);

2) Psychology (how a person thinks);

3) Social (who you spend time with); and

4) Spiritual (what gives your life meaning)."[358]

Daniel Amen believes "that successful psychotherapy, which leads a patient to fresh insights and new cognitive or behavioral patterns, has direct effects on the brain. Learning guides brain development and can produce major changes in brain *hardware*."[359] Understanding the functions of the prefrontal cortex (PFC) thus delves into the brain's hardware. "Good PFC function helps us see ahead of situations – we can get off the train

---

[357] Mental Healthcare Clinic Focusing On Your Brain Health | Dr. Amen. Accessed March 3, 2023. https://www.amenclinics.com/.

[358] Amen, Tana. *The Relentless Courage of a Scared Child: How Persistence, Grit, and Faith Created a Reluctant Healer*. Nashville: Thomas Nelson, 2021. 225.

[359] Amen, Daniel. *Healing the Hardware of the Soul: Enhance Your Brain to Improve Your Work, Love, and Spiritual Life*. New York: Simon & Schuster, 2008. 196.

tracks when we see the train coming. Poor PFC function doesn't allow us to see ahead or plan for the future – we don't see the train until it's about to run over us. For your soul to work right, the PFC must set a good and noble course for you. Your soul must remain on course for spiritual and emotional growth, and it must have the tools to learn from mistakes and follow through on what is profoundly important in your life."[360]

One of the fundamental components of sin is a lack of impulse control, which leads to doing something you know is wrong. "Without full functioning of the PFC, people tend to act on the moment, without forethought or regard for consequences. The PFC translates the feeling of the limbic system, the emotional brain, into recognizable feelings, emotions, and words, such as love, passion, or hate. Underactivity or damage in this part of the brain often leads to a decreased ability to express thoughts and feelings."[361] When there are difficulties in the PFC, daily life becomes difficult to organize, and internal oversight, the conscience, fails.

Shame is rooted in the limbic brain which regulates the non-verbal part of the brain. This results in a startling contradiction of confronting anxieties which forces the limbic system to connect with the PFC. "*Psychotherapy Can Change The Brain.* According to a lecture by Dr. Bernard Beitman of the University of Missouri at Columbia, psychotherapy reroutes signals from the sensory limbic brain that would ordinarily go directly to the amygdala up through the PFC. The result is that patients learn to respond more consciously to external situations or stimuli instead of simply reacting in a habitual, nonadaptive manner."[362]

---

[360] Amen, Daniel. *Healing the Hardware of the Soul: Enhance Your Brain to Improve Your Work, Love, and Spiritual Life.* New York: Simon & Schuster, 2008. 44, 34, 195.

[361] Ibid.
[362] Ibid.

Another study shows "the amygdala retains lasting memories that identify an object and similar objects as dangerous. This is a very powerful and adaptive ability because it allows for the creation of specialized neural circuitry that helps people avoid the specific dangers that occur in their lives."[363] Additionally, "the amygdala's language is based on creating connections between neurons, which brings association, an essential part of the language of the amygdala."[364]

Epigenetics

Addictions can be reversed through the emerging developments in epigenetics. An amalgamation of the brain and the thought life can rewire the brain through meditating on things in the deep subconscious mind that are negative and change the way a person thinks. It is the rumination, the changing of the way one thinks by understanding the role of emotions and feelings that activate or trigger a person.

"In the past two decades, research has revealed that the brain has a surprising level of *neuroplasticity*, meaning an ability to change its structures and reorganize its patterns of reacting. Even parts of the brain that were once thought impossible to change in adults are

---

[363] Pittman, Catherine M., and Elizabeth M. Karle. *Rewire Your Anxious Brain: How to Use the Neuroscience of Fear to End Anxiety, Panic and Worry*. Oakland: New Harbinger Publications Inc, 2015. 38, 43, 6.

[364] Ibid.

capable of being modified, revealing that the brain actually has an amazing capacity to change."[365]

Subsequently, neuroplasticity of the brain can change the way we think about events that once were triggering, to no longer operate as a trigger. Much research and study has been done in this field, to which Dr. Caroline Leaf and Dr. Daniel Amen are two sources that have been highly analyzed for the dismantling of addictive cycles. "This understanding is the result of years of research in a field known as *neuroscience*, which is the science of the structure and function of the nervous system, including the brain."[366] Dr. Leaf has extensive studies on what she has termed as a neurocycle in her book "Cleaning Up The Mental Mess" which will be referred to in the Breaking Cycles section.[367]

Undoubtedly, the brain is not fixed and unalterable, as many people, including scientists, once believed. "The circuits of your brain aren't determined completely by genetics; they're also shaped by your experiences and the way you think and behave. You can remodel your brain to respond differently, no matter what age you are. You can use this information to transform your brain's circuitry so that it resists anxiety, rather than creating it."[368]

The fight, flight, or freeze response is triggered in the amygdala. "When danger is detected, the amygdala can affect a number of highly influential structures in the brain, including the brain stem arousal systems, the hypothalamus, the hippocampus, and the nucleus

---

[365] Ibid.

[366] Pittman, Catherine M., and Elizabeth M. Karle. *Rewire Your Anxious Brain: How to Use the Neuroscience of Fear to End Anxiety, Panic and Worry*. Oakland: New Harbinger Publications Inc, 2015. 5.
[367] Leaf, Caroline. *Cleaning Up Your Mental Mess: 5 Simple, Scientifically Proven Steps to Reduce Anxiety, Stress, and Toxic Thinking*. Ada: Baker Books, 2021.

[368] Pittman, Catherine M., and Elizabeth M. Karle. *Rewire Your Anxious Brain: How to Use the Neuroscience of Fear to End Anxiety, Panic and Worry*. Oakland: New Harbinger Publications Inc, 2015. 6, 41.

accumbens. These direct connections allow the amygdala to instantly activate motor (movement) systems, energize the sympathetic nervous system, increase levels of neurotransmitters, and release hormones like adrenaline and cortisol into the bloodstream."[369] Understanding how hormones impact the brain is an integral part of epigenetics. "The raging residue of stress and trauma is activated in the sympathetic nervous system, which controls most of the body's internal organs, eventually releasing an outpouring of adrenaline, cortisol and other stress-related hormones."[370]

Dopamine

Understanding a few physical aspects of the brain will assist with understanding epigenetics and how to rewire the brain. Dopamine acts as a hormone that "is released into your bloodstream. It plays a small role in the "fight-or-flight" syndrome. The fight-or-flight response refers to your body's response to a perceived or real stressful situation, such as needing to escape danger."[371] Dopamine, along with "epinephrine and norepinephrine are the main catecholamines (a label based on having part of the same molecular structure). These hormones are made by your adrenal gland, a small hat-shaped gland located on top of each of

---

[369] Ibid.

[370] Rogers, Gayle. *The Whole Soul: Rescripting Your Life for Personal Transformation*. Kingdom House Publishing, 2014. 150.

[371] "Dopamine: What It Is, Function & Symptoms." Cleveland Clinic. Last modified March 23, 2023. https://my.clevelandclinic.org/health/articles/22581-dopamine.

your kidneys. Dopamine is also a neurohormone released by the hypothalamus in your brain."[372]

Additionally, understand that "dopamine is a type of monoamine neurotransmitter. It's made in your brain and acts as a chemical messenger, communicating messages between nerve cells in your brain and the rest of your body."[373] Often known as the "feel-good" hormone, dopamine releases a sense of pleasure. "It also gives you the motivation to do something when you're feeling pleasure. Dopamine is part of your reward system."[374]

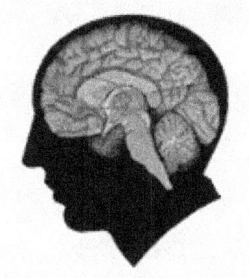
[375]

Yet drugs, often nicknamed *dope,* and these other types of addictions discussed interfere with the way neurons send, receive, and process signals via neurotransmitters. Recreational drugs interfere with the way nerve cells in your brain send and receive messages. Additionally, recreational drugs overstimulate the brain's reward center. "Scientists now think that dopamine's role isn't to directly cause euphoria but serves as a reinforcement for remembering and repeating pleasurable experiences. So, when drugs cause surges in

---

[372] Ibid.
[373] Ibid.
[374] "Dopamine: What It Is, Function & Symptoms." Cleveland Clinic. Last modified March 23, 2023. https://my.clevelandclinic.org/health/articles/22581-dopamine..
[375] Ibid.

dopamine, it's teaching your brain to remember the experience."³⁷⁶ While dopamine is not all destructive, the following illustration will show the difference between normal dopamine emissions, and the use of drugs:

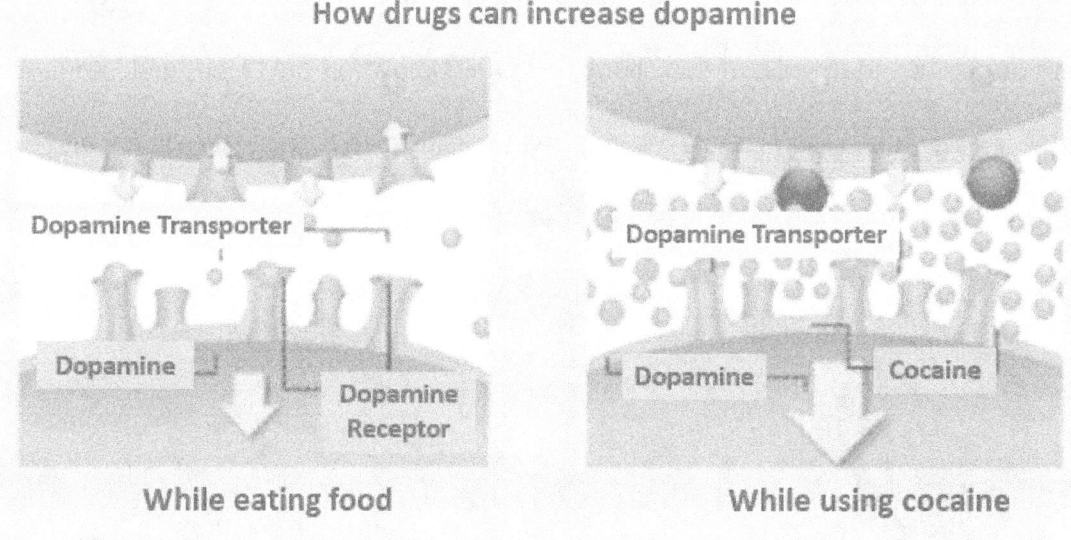

377

---

³⁷⁶ Ibid.

³⁷⁷ "Dopamine: What It Is, Function & Symptoms." Cleveland Clinic. Last modified March 23, 2023. https://my.clevelandclinic.org/health/articles/22581-dopamine.

CHAPTER FOURTEEN: Bodywork

Healing Systems

Your thoughts can cause a molecular change in your brain. Therefore, believers are encouraged to pray over our DNA, and over our body. Our words are so powerful that they can cause a shift and a change in our DNA molecules. Desiree Garland, in her book titled: *Encode: Praying with the language of glory* [378] addresses this phenomenon. We are to pray that God will heal all our systems in our body. The body systems are impacted by the things going on inside of us. My personal testimony as I underwent a hysterectomy in 2009 is that the Lord revealed to me that the fibroid tumors were a result of years of worrying!

Part of healing the systems of the body is to engage in meditative prayer over the following systems for healing:

- Nervous system. Pertains to the brain, spinal cord, and nerves.
- Respiratory system.
- Digestive system. Pertains to the mucous membranes, stomach, pancreas, bladder, bowel.
- Skeletal & Muscular system. Pertains to muscles, bones, joints, connective tissues.

---

[378] Garland, Desiree. *Encode: Praying with the Language of Glory*, 1st ed. Amazon Kindle Direct Publishing, 2020. Kindle edition.

- Immune system. The Protective cells.

- Cardiovascular system.

- Endocrine system. This system often pertains to mental disorders, glands, and hormones. People may need medicine AND Jesus. Not a pill or quick fix, but an awareness of how the systems function.

Believers do not have to accept issues in their body just because they are aging. Some of the problems with these systems is the thought life. Many may be thinking some of those things into manifestation; because as a man thinks, so is he. Hence, many believers are calling those things into manifestation through their thought life. It is a matter of epigenetics; whether you say it out loud or are speaking to your DNA internally.

The Amen Clinics noted that "Psychiatric problems are common after traumatic brain injury, even when the injury is relatively mild. In addition, there is an increased incidence of substance abuse, marital problems, job-related problems, and incarceration and other legal problems."[379]

---

[379] Amen, Daniel. *Healing the Hardware of the Soul: Enhance Your Brain to Improve Your Work, Love, and Spiritual Life*. New York: Simon & Schuster, 2008. 79.

Another Look At Dopamine

The role of understanding body chemistry, considering dopamine highs & lows is part of bodywork. Identifying whether the causes of spikes are by a natural cause or symptom, or by determining what is causing these highs and lows in the physical body is necessary. As believers, we are to be addicted to the presence of God who is our Creator. He will be able to create and stimulate the dopamine levels in the believer better than addictive behaviors or over the counter medications. As discussed earlier, praying over the systems of our body, especially the nervous system are keys to stimulate the natural regulation of hormone levels. Renew the mind to cause the brain to serve as a natural reuptake inhibitor. Allow the Holy Spirit to assist in the Renewal Of The Mind process as we seek the Great Physician.

"How can I improve my dopamine levels in a natural way?" You may wish to try remedies that naturally increase dopamine. Further research is needed on the effects of food on neurotransmitters such as dopamine.

- Eat a diet that's high in magnesium and tyrosine-rich foods. These are the building blocks for dopamine production. Tyrosine is an amino acid. It's absorbed in your body and then goes to your brain, where it's converted into dopamine. Foods known to increase dopamine include chicken, almonds, apples, avocados, bananas, beets, chocolate, green leafy vegetables, green tea, lima beans, oatmeal, oranges, peas, sesame and pumpkin seeds, tomatoes, turmeric, watermelon, and wheat germ.

- Engage in activities that make you happy or feel relaxed. This is thought to increase dopamine levels. Some examples include exercise, meditation, yoga, massage, playing with a pet, walking in nature, or reading a book."[380]

---

[380] "Dopamine: What It Is, Function & Symptoms." Cleveland Clinic. Last modified March 23, 2023. https://my.clevelandclinic.org/health/articles/22581-dopamine.

CHAPTER FIFTEEN: Tool For Renewal Of The Mind

Shane Idleman addressed the topic of *sober but not saved* and stated that an "event motivated me to complete this book and help others find freedom and wholeness, not just sobriety. What does it profit us to gain the world [or find sobriety] yet lose our soul, Mark 8:36."[381] With this in mind, the tool, or system that this thesis proposes will help believers to renew their mind in the quest for identity with a sober, compassionate understanding of freedom and wholeness.

Additionally, Idleman states the following: "It is my firm belief that, second only to salvation, the fully surrendered life is the most important aspect of the Christian life. The fully surrendered life involves humility, dying to self, vibrant prayer, and heartfelt worship – things the average Christian isn't willing to do. This isn't meant to discourage you but to convict, and conviction is a wonderful gift from God used to turn the heart back to Him."[382]

Turn back to Him because love is the drawing force. Kay Tolman adds the following regarding the order of deliverance: "I suggest that we minister love first, before casting out spirits. Care for the child, minister to the wound, then cast out the spirit. Once the wounding is healed, there is no place in the soul for the spirit to attach, and the spirit can be evicted with a whispered command."[383] Let's delve into the elements of this tool to compassionately do just that.

---

[381] Idleman, Shane. *Help! I'm Addicted: Overcoming the Cravings that Overcome You.* El Paseo Publications, 2019. Kindle Edition. 4, 30.

[382] Ibid.

[383] Tolman, Kay. *Moved with Compassion: A New Wineskin for Healing and Deliverance.* 2017. 46.

This Renewal Of The Mind tool can be used individually, by counselors, or in group settings to help with these convictions and will address the following elements: healed emotions; renewed thoughts; breaking cycles; true identity; and healthy coping mechanisms.

<u>Healed Emotions</u>

Emotions must be processed and healed with compassion. Jesus was moved with compassion in Mark chapter five. Compassion will be required to aid someone in transforming their identity, as well as compassion to drive out false identities formed by influences such as those mentioned in the book of Mark. Just like Jesus drove out the legion of spirits, we must drive out whatever is prompting them to engage in addictive behavior. We are to help Jesus by extending our compassion to others. Allow compassion to be a channel that flows to them while not judging them based on one's personal standards or opinions.

A fitting example of this is found in Ephesians 4:26 where it discusses being angry without sin. "What is Paul saying? Experience your anger but don't hurt anyone with it. Don't repress it or hang on to it. Process it today."[384] These real feelings and emotions must be acknowledged and allowed to heal.

Denying one's feelings can be traced back to Stoicism which "implies that feelings are not acceptable or true. Therefore, we deny them, stuff them away and reject our own voice as unacceptable. Unresolved emotions are a breeding ground for addiction. For survivors of

---

[384] Tolman, Kay. *Moved with Compassion: A New Wineskin for Healing and Deliverance*. 2017. 28.

severe trauma and abuse, stoicism hinders recovery and is every bit as abusive as the perpetrator that demands silence. Feelings can be like a light on the dashboard of your car. When people don't acknowledge their deeply held feelings, they can experience physical ailments. There are emotional roots to most physical maladies because the *body speaks for the emotions when they aren't given a voice*.[385] This is why healing the emotions is the first step to acknowledge after receiving the empowerment of the Holy Spirit in the Renewal Of The Mind process toward freedom.

There is a cycle to addiction that must be broken, and it is broken by learning how to deal with the emotional triggers through the Renewal Of The Mind, where the emotions are housed. In His book *Unlocking The Mystery of Your Emotions*, Archibald Hart presents it this way: "The first step toward psychological and physical health is emotional honesty, the ability to recognize and own up to your feelings. The second step is to allow yourself more freedom in the expression of your feelings, with the goal of becoming more *real* emotionally. Only then can you become the master of your emotions and not be a slave to them. Only then can you stop imposing the most demanding and unrealistic expectations on your emotional state and find the freedom to be your true self."[386]

Feelings such as guilt or shame must be dismantled. Keep in mind that "becoming a Christian does not automatically correct psychological guilt problems. It is the application of the resources of the gospel that brings healing."[387] As discussed in a previous chapter, the

---

[385] Tolman, Kay. *Moved with Compassion: A New Wineskin for Healing and Deliverance*. 2017. 29.
[386] Hart, Archibald D. *Unlocking the Mystery of Your Emotions*. W Publishing Group, 1989. 5, 111.
[387] Ibid.

Holy Spirit is a great resource for applying the gospel of truth to one's life to experience this type of emotional freedom.

Here is another aspect to absorb regarding emotions: one must gain "a revelation concerning the importance of elevated emotion as the carrier wave of God's healing power. Spirit-born emotions which carry the power to heal! What a concept! The kingdom of God is the emotions of peace and joy, and the fruit of the Spirit includes emotions of love, joy, and peace (See Romans 14:17, Galatians 5:22). These are Spirit-born emotions, or kingdom emotions"[388]

Prayer is a powerful tool as it relates to healing emotions. An "abbot was sharing the instructions that describe how we can speak the language of quantum possibilities, and he was doing so through a technique that we know today as a form of prayer. No wonder prayers work miracles! They put us in touch with the pure space where the miracles of our minds become the reality of our world."[389] Compassionate prayer is a powerful combination. *Compassion: A Force of Nature and a Human Experience.* "For our prayers to be answered, we must transcend the doubt that often accompanies the positive nature of our desire."[390]

Lastly, Greg Braden discussed renewing the understanding of a common scripture found in John 16:23-24 of the King James Version Bible. When he compared "this with the original text, we see the key that's left out. In the following paragraph, I've emphasized the missing part by underlining it. '*All things that you ask straightly, directly ... from inside My*

---

[388] Tolman, Kay. *Moved with Compassion: A New Wineskin for Healing and Deliverance.* 2017. 5.

[389] Braden, Gregg. *The Divine Matrix: Bridging Time, Space, Miracles, and Belief.* Carlsbad: Hay House, 2007. 85.

[390] Ibid.

name – you will be given. So far you haven't done this ... So, ask without hidden motive and be surrounded by your answer – Be enveloped by what you desire, that your gladness be full. With these words, we're reminded of the quantum principle telling us that feeling is a language to direct and focus our consciousness. It's a state of being that we're *in*, rather than something that we *do* at a certain time of day."[391] Prayer and these healed emotions and feelings are a crucial part of the tool of Renewal Of The Mind.

Renewed Thoughts

Gayle Rogers shares the following about renewed thoughts: "To activate the untapped power within your DNA requires you to get in touch with your inner self, not looking for someone else to legitimize or authenticate your identity. Learning how to do healing work on myself, discovering my own emotions and how to change my old thinking patterns, has been a rewarding adventure, literally changing my life."[392]

Be renewed in the spirit of your mind: the dichotomy of Renewal Of The Mind. Be like the man in Luke 8:35, who was found sitting at the feet of Jesus, clothed and in a right, sound mind. "Don't get stuck in past mindsets formed through disappointments or failures. Renew your mind and start thinking like God. The more you believe like Him, the more you

---

[391] Braden, Gregg. *The Divine Matrix: Bridging Time, Space, Miracles, and Belief.* Carlsbad: Hay House, 2007. 88.

[392] Rogers, Gayle. *The Whole Soul: Rescripting Your Life for Personal Transformation.* Kingdom House Publishing, 2014. 93.

will become like Him."[393] Attitudes must be renewed and adjusted. "An attitude is thus a 'preprogrammed' response to a given action."[394]

When these 'programs' are renewed, thoughts are renewed. "Our thoughts become words, our words become actions, our actions become habits. Who or what is shaping your thoughts?"[395] The progression is evident in a calm renewed mind. "Calmness of mind is one of the beautiful jewels of wisdom. It is the result of long and patient effort in self-control. Its presence is an indication of ripened experience, and of a more than ordinary knowledge of the laws and operations of thought."[396]

We have looked at the role of the brain in the first portion of this project, it is beneficial to have a better understanding of the parts of the brain that influence the thought life. "The area of the brain that experiences emotion is also the area of the brain through which we experience God. The new wineskin for healing and deliverance requires us to intimately know Him so we can minister in and through His presence. In the process, we must learn how to care for emotions."[397]

This revelation can be helpful with breaking cycles and walking in true identity with healthy coping mechanisms. "The things we believe, the emotions we feel, the trauma that seeks resolution, is all in the right brain. You can read about God and not know Him. Or you can experience Him with your spirit and soul and be forever changed. The most effective

---

[393] Alger, Wanda. *Oracles of Grace: Building a Legacy of Wisdom and Revelation*. Alger Publications, 2017. 97.
[394] Hart, Archibald D. *Unlocking the Mystery of Your Emotions*. W Publishing Group, 1989. 33.
[395] Idleman, Shane. *Help! I'm Addicted: Overcoming the Cravings that Overcome You*. El Paseo Publications, 2019. Kindle Edition. 55.
[396] Allen, James. *As a Man Thinketh*. Amazon, 2014. Kindle Edition. 32.
[397] Tolman, Kay. *Moved with Compassion: A New Wineskin for Healing and Deliverance*. 2017. 35, 40.

ministry activates the capacity of the right hemisphere of the brain where Jesus Himself does the healing of the broken heart."[398]

Breaking Cycles

Cycles must be broken with the help of the Holy Spirit. "Those addicted can't simply say, 'I'm going to simply let go and let God,' without also applying the principles found in His Word."[399] The cycles weren't formed overnight, and they may not be healed overnight. "As stated earlier, to get out from under bondage a Renewal Of The Mind must take place and that only comes with a long-term relationship with Jesus."[400]

God will do what seems impossible. "Do not remain broken; make a decision to trust your past and your future to the Lord."[401] One must work out their own salvation as in Philippians 2:12. This process is "described by Thayer's Lexicon as soteria, meaning deliverance from the molestation of enemies. Although the atoning blood of Jesus delivered our spirit-man from the power of Satan, it is the responsibility of the believer to work out his or her own deliverance from the molestation of enemies, freeing both the soul and body."[402] Believers have a role to play in the their own healing, which is "the miracle of God's recycling

---

[398] Ibid.
[399] Idleman, Shane. *Help! I'm Addicted: Overcoming the Cravings that Overcome You*. El Paseo Publications, 2019. Kindle Edition. 14.

[400] Rogers, Gayle. *Healing The Traumatized Soul*. AuthorHouse, 2005. 118.
[401] Meyer, Joyce. *Beauty for Ashes: Receiving Emotional Healing*. Fenton: FaithWords, 2003. 222.
[402] Rogers, Gayle. *Healing The Traumatized Soul*. AuthorHouse, 2005. 97.

grace, where He takes it all and makes good come out of it, where He actually recycles our hangups into wholeness and usefulness."[403]

Breaking cycles, deliverance, and achieving this wholeness and usefulness may come in stages. The initial stage is being born again and the second stage is making the decision to take responsibility for one's own life. A relationship with Christ must be established as a way of life rather than something that is only done during times of trouble. "If they can unlearn the behavior of negatively reacting to every negative situation, they can acquire the skills to keep the enemy from continuing to entrap them."[404]

This tool also enforces the need for discipleship and community as an essential element for breaking cycles because "Jesus gave the church the power to trample the evil treachery, craftiness, deception, scheming and venom of serpents as in Luke 10:18."[405]

Relapsing into addictive behaviors can be halted by understanding this acronym for the word **HALT**: **H**ungry, **A**ngry, **L**onely, or **T**ired."[406] Many normal life conditions can act as triggers that will cause a person to lapse back into the vicious cycle of addictive behavior. One person shared their process as that it took a while to adjust, yet "by the time we left, my thinking had been cracked open. I wasn't magically fixed, but I was open to new possibilities and ready to begin the healing process."[407]

---

[403] Seamands, David A. *Healing for Damaged Emotions*. Wheaton: David C Cook, 1991. 139.
[404] Rogers, Gayle. *Healing The Traumatized Soul*. AuthorHouse, 2005. 108, 107.

[405] Ibid.

[406] Idleman, Shane. *Help! I'm Addicted: Overcoming the Cravings that Overcome You*. El Paseo Publications, 2019. Kindle Edition. 165.
[407] Amen, Tana. *The Relentless Courage of a Scared Child: How Persistence, Grit, and Faith Created a Reluctant Healer*. Nashville: Thomas Nelson, 2021. 167-168.

Reality living, as Dr. Gary Chapman explains, is a vital step in breaking any type of cycle in one's life. "The basic principles of reality living are:

1) I am responsible for my own attitude.

2) My attitude affects my actions.

3) I cannot change others, but I can influence others.

4) My emotions do NOT control my actions.

5) Admitting my imperfections does not mean that I am a failure.

6) Love is the most powerful weapon for good in the world."[408]

Lastly, Gayle Rogers offers some beginning steps to achieving freedom that when combined with Gary Chapman's list above are a double portion way to dislodge cycles and walk in freedom. "The following seven steps will help abused women achieve the freedom to be who they have been called to be:

1. The desire and resolve to be totally free must be stronger than any other desire except a desire for a deeper relationship with Christ.

2. Getting an understanding of spiritual warfare and looking only to the power of the Holy Spirit for total deliverance.

3. A willingness to let go of the anger and forgive the perpetrator.

4. Developing a right relationship with Christ.

---

[408] Chapman, Gary D. *Desperate Marriages: Moving Toward Hope and Healing in Your Relationship*. Chicago: Northfield Pub, 2008. 51.

5. The ability to identify and acknowledge ancestral sins/hurts (which encompasses aftereffects such as anger, self-worthlessness, offense, depression, rejection, unforgiveness, idolatry, bitterness, etc.), renounce them and move on.
6. A desire to be made whole according to Matthew 9:21 and John 5:6.
7. A recognition that there is a stronghold over those who violated you and *pray* for their deliverance (if they are still living), because they too are in bondage and need to be released."[409]

True Identity

Only God can give a person their self-worth, it is not possible for another human being to successfully do this. "Identifying with Christ gives an individual a makeover opportunity which lasts a lifetime; ever evolving into the image of the Godhead. Simply stated, this means your identity is not based on how others treat you or life experiences. Instead, the core of who you are is *so* deeply rooted in the love and faithfulness of God that you can give and share of yourself without losing your God-given value."[410] This is paramount to a healthy identity.

We must know our identity as well as our Heavenly Father. "If we see God as the 'Great Punisher,' our relationship with Him becomes one of fear and guilt rather than one of

---

[409] Rogers, Gayle. *Healing The Traumatized Soul*. AuthorHouse, 2005. 123.

[410] Dillon, Brandy, and Dionne Davis. *Come Forth: Transformational Principles to Arise from Life's Afflictions*. Raleigh: PENDIUM, 2018. 30.

love and trust. If our faith *increases guilt* rather than *decreases guilt*, we have a legalistic, rules-based relationship with God. The more we recognize God's undeserved forgiveness for our wrong choices – the more we will seek to please God by making choices that are right in His sight."[411] This increases the Screwtape Element by the incorrect perception of guilt.

When we understand that our worth is based on our identity in Christ rather than our achievements or conduct, we are then able to shift our minds from what others are thinking about us all the time and have the confidence to simply be ourselves. "Confidence has been defined as the quality of assurance that leads one to undertake something; the belief that one is able and acceptable; the certainty that causes one to be bold, open, and plain."[412]

Renewing the mind to understanding confidence according to these three points and the continual understanding that God loves you regardless of what has happened to you or what you do is the goal. The adversary is working against us from the womb to tarnish identity.

Some children may never have been abused, but they were raised by parents who were. This will help us understand future generations that appear to lack a sense of pride and awareness; it is due to broken people (parents) raising people (children), passing on generational trauma in the emotions, without the actual traumatic experience itself. If while you were growing up you did not receive what you needed to make you sound and healthy, Jesus will gladly give it to you now. Renew your mind through the transferred anger of previous generations, to the truth about your identity and some of the peculiarities that operate in life, recognizing the Screwtape Element of distorting confidence.

---

[411] Hunt, June. *Guilt: Living Guilt-Free*. Peabody: Aspire Press, 2013. 42.
[412] Meyer, Joyce. *Beauty for Ashes: Receiving Emotional Healing*. Fenton: FaithWords, 2003. 114, 120.

Confidence to be an Individual. Don't Try to be Someone Else. "Remember this: God said that we 'shall not covet' in Exodus 20:17, and that includes someone else's personality."[413] This makes a valid point in the Renewal of the Mind process since many people don't look at it as coveting, or maybe regard it as self-improvement or some form of flattery which leads to lost identity. Note, the plumbline for self-improvement is the Bible, not other people.

Identity is patterned after Jesus. "Through both tragedies and triumphs, I have learned that Jesus is my King, and He wants to be yours, too. The kingdom He desires to reign over is our inner life – our mind, will, emotions, desires, and thoughts."[414] Walk in the fullness of salvation and identity to not have the following testimony: "Legally, I was a new creature in Christ; but experientially, I had not yet taken hold of the new creation reality. I lived out of my own mind, will, and emotions, which were all damaged. Jesus had paid the price for my total deliverance, but I had no idea how to receive His gracious gift."[415] *Just receive the gift.*

"Refusal to embrace your God-given identity can lead to a curse; therefore, removing the distortions is imperative. Distortions are false identifications or thought processes of something, someone, or of yourself; lies. God knows how to locate you. If you make yourself available to the exposure, extraction, and renewal process, He will shine His light on every area of your life and dismantle the lies of the enemy. The lies of the enemy can enter someone's life through labels, limitations, and loneliness, to name a few."[416]

---

[413] Ibid.
[414] Meyer, Joyce. *Beauty for Ashes: Receiving Emotional Healing.* Fenton: FaithWords, 2003. 4, 24.
[415] Ibid.
[416] Dillon, Brandy, and Dionne Davis. *Come Forth: Transformational Principles to Arise from Life's Afflictions.* Raleigh: PENDIUM, 2018. 47.

In closing this section, I'd like to share a prayer I found regarding salvation and identity: "**Prayer:** Lord God I welcome You to live inside my heart. Cleanse it, heal it, and guard it from unrighteousness and deception that tries to stain my identity in You. No matter what I experience in this life, I believe I am valuable. I believe You are willing and able to use my life. Forgive me for not trusting in You and trying to do things my way. I want Your perfect will to be done in every area of my life. Help me by the power of Your Spirit to do the good works You predestined for my life. In Jesus' name I pray. Amen."[417]

Healthy Coping Mechanisms

We must have healthy coping mechanisms, which is another way of saying addiction, or habit, or habitual behavior. These mindsets must be renewed daily; instead of resorting to unhealthy mindsets which lead to the previous addiction of choice, instead turn to:

- The Holy Spirit, The Helper, The Spirit of Truth.
- Be addicted to trusting God amidst all situations and not get caught up in anxieties.

The opposite of coping mechanisms are defense mechanisms. "What comes out of our mouths is often the fruit of defense mechanisms that we subconsciously employ as our fleshly nature wages war against the truth of the Kingdom of God. Defense mechanisms mask the

---

[417] Dillon, Brandy, and Dionne Davis. *Come Forth: Transformational Principles to Arise from Life's Afflictions*. Raleigh: PENDIUM, 2018. 44.

pain we feel inwardly, so that we are incapable of acknowledging it, working through it, and moving on. The enemy knows the power of inner distraction and tries to keep us bound up in lie-based thinking that is contrary to the liberating principles of God's Word."[418] Another Screwtape Element exposed!

The soul healing principles of forgiveness, connection, giving to others, focused thoughts, and leaving judgement to the Almighty are profound coping strategies along with faith, trust, love, joy, and discipline. "The pain of discipline is temporary, while the pain of regret lingers."[419] Hence, believers are encouraged to have the mental discipline to forget the past, but not the lessons learned. "To be healed isn't the same as being cured. But to be healed is to feel mended – whole again after being broken."[420]

Keep pressing toward a healthy mental state knowing that "God honors perseverance, not perfection."[421] Our beliefs are continually being shaped and tested. An acronym for **BELIEVE** is: "**B**ecause **E**mmanuel **L**ives **I** **E**xpect **V**ictory **E**very-time."[422] Our identity is in Emmanuel, God with us, we can handle the many revelations He will be revealing to us as in second Corinthians 12 which discusses the role of revelations and the accompanying grace. Revelation is God revealing things to you, the mystery is you growing and stretching in your capacity to walk in that which has been revealed.

---

[418] Stearns, Robert. *The Cry of Mordecai: Awakening an Esther Generation in a Haman Age*. Shippensburg: Destiny Image Pub, 2009. 53.

[419] Idleman, Shane. *Help! I'm Addicted: Overcoming the Cravings that Overcome You*. El Paseo Publications, 2019. Kindle Edition. 60.

[420] Amen, Tana. *The Relentless Courage of a Scared Child: How Persistence, Grit, and Faith Created a Reluctant Healer*. Nashville: Thomas Nelson, 2021. 224.

[421] Idleman, Shane. *Help! I'm Addicted: Overcoming the Cravings that Overcome You*. El Paseo Publications, 2019. Kindle Edition. 83.

[422] Dillon, Brandy, and Dionne Davis. *Come Forth: Transformational Principles to Arise from Life's Afflictions*. Raleigh: PENDIUM, 2018. 57, 59.

"Let go of the lies and labels so you can experience His love, His peace, His confidence, His presence. You will need all of this for your journey. Welcome His resurrecting and restoring power into every area of your life you thought was dead; you won't be disappointed."[423] The following section lists several areas to adapt healthy coping strategies: bibliotherapy, love, joy, humility, forgiveness, authenticity, prayer, obedience, and meekness.

Bibliotherapy

Bibliotherapy involves using or assigning books related to these topics for one to read, journal about, and bring for discussion regarding what they found interesting. This can be done in a group setting, or as a follow up to counseling. Oftentimes it is necessary to re-read books to pick up on other items covered in the book yet overlooked. Again, the goal is Bible-based books, because the word of God is active and living, and the book will mean different things at contrasting times in life. Kay Tolman believes that "the Word of God is authoritative and the basis for truth. Scripture is more than mere words on a page; it has a transforming power that brings Renewal Of The Mind, body, soul, and spirit.[424]

Bibliotherapy can be like having the author with you as a friend. This is my personal coping mechanism, to do recorded audio exhortations of my studies and various books that I would go back to and listen regularly. This practice has helped me through a lot of depressive or anxious life events. Either creating the recordings, or listening to the recordings, which are

---
[423] Ibid.
[424] Tolman, Kay. *Moved with Compassion: A New Wineskin for Healing and Deliverance*. 2017. 13.

both beneficial coping mechanisms. This may not work for everyone, but it is what has proven to work for me. While experiencing trauma in my childhood I would hide by reading books, it was my escape. Now, what the devil meant for evil has proven to be the very thing that God is using for my good, and the good of many others.

A powerful book suggestion is Dr. Caroline Leaf's book *Cleaning Up The Mental Mess* which can assist with understanding and reprogramming the mind using what she has defined as neurocycles. Yet another reference is Bill Gillham's book *Lifetime Guarantee – Making Your Christian Life Work and What to Do When It Doesn't*.[425] He has a section that shows "how to apply the four-step sequence of truth, faith, works and emotions to develop a technique for walking in the Spirit rather than *according to the flesh*[426] which is extremely helpful with establishing healthy coping mechanisms. Any of the books from the bibliography of this project can be assigned depending on the presenting life mindsets that need to be renewed.

YouTube can be used as a bibliotherapy tool also. The goal is to assign specific playlist or trusted individuals to follow and learn more about the biblical Renewal of the Mind process, and the other areas of healthy coping mechanisms that will be discussed.

---

[425] Gillham, Bill. *Lifetime Guarantee*. Eugene: Harvest House Pub, 1993. 163.

[426] Ibid.

Love

One must renew the mind to the definition and meaning of love and how it is foundational when dealing with addictive behaviors. As seen earlier, love is our first basic need, along with acceptance. It is critical to be reminded that Jesus fulfills the law, which is the law of love. "Love is the pesticide to any unwanted contents in any area of your lives, for love covers a multitude of sins, 1 Peter 4:8."[427] Additionally, believers are encouraged to mature in love as in 1 Corinthians 13 verse 11.

"We must not forget that the mind – as well as the heart, soul, and strength – is vital to loving the Lord."[428] Hence, the need to renew the mind to accurately view our roles and think with clarity according to Mark 12:30. "God's love is the greatest issue in which people need to have a revelation. People do not need a teaching about the love of God as much as they need to personally experience and understand how much God loves them as an individual."[429] Or as Kay Tolman has said: "We need a baptism of love and compassion so we can walk as Jesus walked and move as Jesus moved."[430] Taken a step further, one must answer the question that Bob Jones often asked people: "*Did you learn to love?* Because love, the currency of heaven, changes things here on earth."[431]

Also, because "love is irresistible. It always conquers. There is no way it can be defeated. Love protects us from all negative forces like resentment, unforgiveness, bitterness,

---

[427] Dillon, Brandy, and Dionne Davis. *Come Forth: Transformational Principles to Arise from Life's Afflictions*. Raleigh: PENDIUM, 2018. 41.
[428] Prince, Derek. *Pulling Down Strongholds*. Charlotte: Whitaker House, 2013. 62.
[429] Meyer, Joyce. *Beauty for Ashes: Receiving Emotional Healing*. Fenton: FaithWords, 2003. 188.
[430] Tolman, Kay. *Moved with Compassion: A New Wineskin for Healing and Deliverance*. 2017. 14, 23.
[431] Ibid.

discouragement, and despair that can corrupt our hearts and spoil our lives."[432] This is like the heart brain coherence concept and tapping into compassion, one cannot have judgement in their heart, therefore one must meditate on the love of God.

Misconceptions about love exists and often can lead to depression. "Hippocrates gives prominence to problems of love as a cause of depression, and both the Greeks and Romans held the view that all depression was caused by disappointments in love."[433] These disappointments can form in childhood. Hence, the early roots of love problems, and deception. Some people believe that God's love for us is conditional on our worthiness, this "is a deception that causes many problems in our lives. On the other hand, believing that God loves us unconditionally brings much joy and blessedness."[434]

To compensate for childhood love inadequacies, "many will resort to defensive strategies and their subsequent personalities, to a large extent, are shaped by and reflect these strategies. When a person who is deprived of love for a prolonged period during the first or second years of life, they can become psychologically stunted."[435] Those with an underdeveloped understanding of love may develop addictive behaviors. "Of the most serious but still disturbing ways in which we try to cope with love deprivation the following are the most common:

1. A tendency to seek for love: people pleasing; being a clingy person; developing love substitutes.

---

[432] Prince, Derek. *Spiritual Warfare*. Charlotte: Whitaker House, 2001. 64.
[433] Hart, Archibald D. *Unlocking the Mystery of Your Emotions*. W Publishing Group, 1989. 76.
[434] Meyer, Joyce. *Beauty for Ashes: Receiving Emotional Healing*. Fenton: FaithWords, 2003. 43.
[435] Hart, Archibald D. *Unlocking the Mystery of Your Emotions*. W Publishing Group, 1989. 132.

2. The development of severe character traits which are deeply stamped into one's personality: excessive jealousy; self-pity; sexual immorality; pervasive insecurity.

3. The creation of pain or illness to handle love deprivation."[436]

To add on to this last concept above, many people develop addictions to mask love deprivation.

Joy

A hallmark of a mature life is a continual state of joy, regardless of all circumstances. The paradox of joy is present in all circumstances, whether favorable or not. However, it is interesting how Scripture clearly identifies some of the obstacles to a life of joy:

- "Worldly cares, Matthew 13:22.
- Life's circumstances, Psalm 126:5.
- Worry and anxiety, John 14:27.
- Hurried lifestyle, Proverbs 19:2."[437]

---

[436] Hart, Archibald D. *Unlocking the Mystery of Your Emotions*. W Publishing Group, 1989. 133, 145.

[437] Ibid.

One of the most misunderstood emotions is joy, as many people seek joy through worldly pursuits or pleasures. However, true joy is found in the Lord Jesus Christ, or as the Old Testament says, "The joy of the Lord is your strength (Nehemiah 8:10 KJV)." Furthermore, joy should be the central focus of every Christian's life. "Joy and *being* go together. They are inseparable. By *being* I mean being grounded in Christ, being rooted in the source of all joy. There is no real deep joy outside of this grounding."[438]

Tana Amen explains how dismantling addictive behaviors and acquiring her God-given purpose brought her much joy: "In helping myself learn to use food as medicine, I had discovered my true purpose: to help others heal with food. The most enlightening thing I learned about food is how it affects hormones and mood, how food is instrumental in treating anxiety, depression, ADHD – even eating disorders. As a result, teaching people about the connection between food, mood, and brain health became my mission."[439] This mission brought her much joy!

Humility

Self-humbling is crucial to the Renewal Of The Mind process. "Ask yourself: 'Would I continue this destructive habit if I never got caught?' if the answer is yes, then you have not

---

[438] Hart, Archibald D. *Unlocking the Mystery of Your Emotions*. W Publishing Group, 1989. 145.

[439] Amen, Tana. *The Relentless Courage of a Scared Child: How Persistence, Grit, and Faith Created a Reluctant Healer*. Nashville: Thomas Nelson, 2021. 189.

humbled yourself and fully repented."[440] Humility is about balance and will require the assistance of the Holy Spirit, the Counselor Himself, providing strength within and assisting with the transformation into the image of God.

Allow God to fill your empty heart. Joyce Meyer explains the process of humility she experienced in early life: "I needed daily fixes of self-worth, just like an addict craves his drugs. People who have a root of rejection in their life feel unloved and insecure. Their personality is broken; they are shattered inside. As a result, they are constantly looking for something to make them feel okay. The Holy Spirit is the only One ordained to do a work within us."[441] It is by gaining assertiveness, that one can be helped to "balance God-pleasing humility with God-pleasing self-esteem so that you honor the rights of others while you honor yourself."[442]

Forgiveness

In short, "f*orgiveness* is the key to giving up your need to hurt back. *Forgiveness* is the antidote for hurt anger. There is no other satisfactory solution to our urge to take revenge. Therefore, forgiveness is surrendering my right to hurt you back if you hurt me."[443] At the core of understanding forgiveness is understanding that God calls us to be forgivers.

---

[440] Idleman, Shane. *Help! I'm Addicted: Overcoming the Cravings that Overcome You*. El Paseo Publications, 2019. Kindle Edition. 33.

[441] Meyer, Joyce. *Beauty for Ashes: Receiving Emotional Healing*. Fenton: FaithWords, 2003. 200.

[442] Koch, Ruth N., and Kenneth C. Haugk. *Speaking the Truth in Love: How to be an Assertive Christian*. St Louis: Stephen Ministries St Louis, 1992. 70.

[443] Hart, Archibald D. *Unlocking the Mystery of Your Emotions*. W Publishing Group, 1989. 65, 58.

The following topics are some areas of Renewal of the Mind pertaining to forgiveness:

- A divine perspective towards sin.
  - Be conscious, aware, then our conscience will convict us, and we will repent.
- Renewed towards pain. Renewed about forgiveness – because both are decisions.
  - Be addicted to forgiveness – receive it – and extend it.
  - Because unforgiveness opens a door (portal, entryway) for demonic influence. Which can be masked by holding a grudge, that is an addiction, it is causing chemicals to be released in our body. That is why they say that unforgiveness is like drinking poison and hoping the other person dies. You are poisoning your body and your soul through bitterness and unforgiveness.
  - Let's be addicted to forgiveness.
- Let's decide to receive the help of the Holy Spirit and be freed from addictions as we go through and renew our mind. Addictions will have to let us go!!! God gets the glory!

When we really understand the forgiveness of God, we receive forgiveness for ourselves, and extend it to others. Dr. Archibald Hart states that: "Forgiveness is at the heart of the Christian gospel. It is the 'genius' and exclusive domain of Christianity, and not without reason. God knows who and what we are, and He has given and demonstrated forgiveness in a remarkable way. He knows that we need to both give and receive forgiveness. As a psychologist I am convinced that to know both how to receive and give forgiveness is crucial to the problem of anger. No person is emotionally or spiritually mature who has not mastered the art of forgiving."[444] A mark of a renewed mind is the capacity to operate in mature forgiveness, with the evidence of being able to receive and extend forgiveness.

Notwithstanding the importance of forgiveness in the Christian gospel, guilt issues are common among Christians. "The foundation for these problems is laid in early childhood. It is possible to come into adulthood with an overdeveloped or an underdeveloped system of guilt. An abnormally sensitive conscience can give rise to guilt feelings that: 1) Do not respond to forgiveness (whether from people or God); 2) Do not cause us to make constructive amends; and 3) Are the product of moralism (concern for surface behavior) and not morality."[445]

Forgiveness is good for your soul and your brain. "Anger and resentment cause an increased production of the body's stress hormone, cortisol. In the short run, cortisol makes you feel sped up, tense, and overwhelmed. In the long run, heightened cortisol levels impair the immune system, making you more likely to become ill, and damage cells in the memory centers of the brain. New brain research has demonstrated that excess cortisol levels impair cognitive ability. Learning how to forgive and let go of the negative feelings you harbor has a healing effect on your overall well-being."[446] What an essential element of the tool of Renewal Of The Mind!

---

[444] Hart, Archibald D. *Unlocking the Mystery of Your Emotions*. W Publishing Group, 1989. 122.
[445] Ibid. 122.

[446] Amen, Daniel. *Healing the Hardware of the Soul: Enhance Your Brain to Improve Your Work, Love, and Spiritual Life*. New York: Simon & Schuster, 2008. 252.

Grace is an accompanying element in the forgiveness process. "Grace is the power of the Holy Spirit that comes to us to help us accomplish God's will."[447] It is through grace that one can handle being mistreated or misunderstood. "What matters more than the mistreatment, misunderstanding, or unforgiveness of others is how *you* respond. Will you allow it to affect you as poison or will you use it as fuel to reflect God's character?"[448]

Forgiveness takes place in the heart first and doesn't always require face-to-face interaction with the person whom you extend forgiveness to. The heart is where bitterness flows, it is where the kingdom should be; yet it can be blocked and obstructed by bitterness. Choose to release their sins against you; forgiveness frees you to live again. "Receiving forgiveness for past mistakes and sins, and forgiving others for their mistakes and sins, are two of the most important factors in emotional healing."[449]

Authenticity

Dr. Archibald Hart describes some key characteristics of a real person are "authenticity, integrity, and adaptability."[450] As well as the following barriers to becoming real: "beliefs and expectations; and an unsatisfactory environment."[451]

---

[447] Meyer, Joyce. *Beauty for Ashes: Receiving Emotional Healing*. Fenton: FaithWords, 2003. 137.
[448] Dillon, Brandy, and Dionne Davis. *Come Forth: Transformational Principles to Arise from Life's Afflictions*. Raleigh: PENDIUM, 2018. 23.

[449] Meyer, Joyce. *Beauty for Ashes: Receiving Emotional Healing*. Fenton: FaithWords, 2003. 125.
[450] Hart, Archibald D. *Unlocking the Mystery of Your Emotions*. W Publishing Group, 1989. 153, 157.
[451] Ibid.

Dr. Hart noted "three conditions that had to be present for people to become *real* or fully authentic. These conditions should be present in childhood. If they are not, that child grows up with some distortion of his or her real self. These conditions are: 1) Unconditional acceptance and warmth; 2) Empathic understanding; and 3) Congruence or genuineness.

"These qualities *heal* people, so much so that he calls them the *therapeutic triad*. They provide a nonthreatening atmosphere in which people can explore and develop their true selves. Whenever relationships are characterized by these conditions and whenever communities foster these traits among their members, people are transformed from being artificial and phony into real people."[452] Real people require "authentic love that will not enable, it doesn't ignore problems, but will confront sin. Love doesn't demand its own way, but respects choices. True love is unconditional, accepting, and rare."[453] True love is authentic.

Prayer

Prayer is communication with God, and the best prayer language is to pray the word of God. Pausing and acknowledging God's presence is the essence of prayer, not necessarily coming with a laundry list of requests and things needed. Bibliotherapy with books regarding prayer can help to enhance one's prayer life and build confidence in praying scripturally. Daniel Amen says: "From my perspective as a psychiatrist and brain researcher, there are a

---

[452] Hart, Archibald D. *Unlocking the Mystery of Your Emotions*. W Publishing Group, 1989. 150.
[453] Tolman, Kay. *Moved with Compassion: A New Wineskin for Healing and Deliverance*. 2017. 23.

number of reasons why prayer and meditative states help patients. Prayer and meditation teach us to focus and quiet our minds. They encourage mindful discipline."[454]

Which discipline, as seen several places in this project, is a helpful tool for the Renewal Of The Mind. The benefits and effects of disciplined prayer and meditation can be seen when considering brain scans as performed at the Amen Clinic. "The common theme of the scans is an overall enhancement of prefrontal cortex PFC activity because the brain is more focused, with decreased anterior cingulate, basal ganglia, and limbic activity. This evidence shows that the brain is calmer, less anxious, more relaxed, and more positive during the meditative state."[455] This meditative state is achieved through prayer.

Obedience And Meekness

Meekness is a companion of obedience. Another way of saying meek, is to say calm, which are both elements of a self-controlled obedient spirit. "Self-control is strength; Right Thought is mastery; Calmness is power. Say unto your heart: 'Peace, be still'!"[456] Sanctification is forged in the stillness of one's heart. Yet sanctification is God's job, while obedience is ours. Obedience is a choice of the will.

---

[454] Amen, Daniel. *Healing the Hardware of the Soul: Enhance Your Brain to Improve Your Work, Love, and Spiritual Life*. New York: Simon & Schuster, 2008. 198, 199.

[455] Ibid.

[456] Allen, James. *As a Man Thinketh*. Amazon, 2014. Kindle Edition. 33.

"The Hebrew meaning of obedience adds the concept that a meek person isn't quickly or easily angered but knows the right time and the right cause for anger."[457] Therefore, a meek and obedient person knows how to handle anger, which is according to the fruit of love. "Jesus called His people to move beyond the Old Testament laws of revenge to the higher law of love."[458]

Be willing to sow love. SOW: **S**ubmit, **O**bey and be **W**illing to let the Lord be glorified through your life experiences. As Tana Amen has said: "The experience would teach me a powerful lesson: sometimes God calls us to help those we don't want to help so He can provide healing for the broken parts of us."[459] Sow into other's recovery and Renewal Of The Mind process.

---

[457] Koch, Ruth N., and Kenneth C. Haugk. *Speaking the Truth in Love: How to be an Assertive Christian*. St Louis: Stephen Ministries St Louis, 1992. 75, 71.

[458] Ibid.

[459] Amen, Tana. *The Relentless Courage of a Scared Child: How Persistence, Grit, and Faith Created a Reluctant Healer*. Nashville: Thomas Nelson, 2021. 11.

CHAPTER SIXTEEN: Summary and Conclusions

In summary, "there are four things to do when trouble and trials come to you: 1) Stay emotionally stable; 2) Trust God; 3) Pray immediately to avoid getting into fear; and 4) Keep doing good. The fifth thing to do is expect a reward."[460]

Once one's mind has been renewed, he or she will be able to follow these things when encountering trouble and trials. "To encourage your faith to press on to the higher prize of freedom from emotional pain, God has included many stories of victory in the Bible to remind you of people who learned to shake off offenses and remain faithful to the Lord."[461] Again, a bibliotherapy assignment could be to locate these stories and characters that relate to you individually and study in depth for Renewal Of The Mind.

Part one of this project delved into the aspect of Renewal Of The Mind, beginning with understanding the realms of the mind. We defined the difference between the mind and the soul. Early formation was addressed and how the mind is programmed at an early age. Next, we reviewed the difference between conscience and conscious, being aware and morality, which leads to understanding the role of guilt.

The thought life and strongholds were defined as part of the Renewal Of The Mind process. Feelings and emotions were described and chapter one concluded with a Biblical survey of the various types of minds that are found in the Bible.

Chapter two introduced the role of the Holy Spirit that He plays in being the revealer of truth and exposing lies and deception that need to be dismantled and getting in alignment

---

[460] Meyer, Joyce. *Beauty for Ashes: Receiving Emotional Healing*. Fenton: FaithWords, 2003. 230, 235.

[461] Ibid.

with truth. Next, we looked at the difference between the mind versus the brain and the science of the brain including how the brain functions with communication and perception.

Chapter four included guidelines for transformation that will assist in the Renewal Of The Mind. Then we arrived at part two of the thesis, looking at the dichotomy of addictions by delving into the probable causes of addiction which we saw as: demonic influence; passiveness or aggressiveness; unresolved anger; trauma; damaged emotions; memory repression; conflict avoidance; depression; and denial. The next section surveyed several types of addiction, followed by chapter seven which discussed the functioning of the brain and addictions, concluding with how epigenetics and the role of dopamine impact the Renewal Of The Mind process.

Chapter eight discussed bodywork, looking at healing the systems of the body, followed by another look at dopamine and how it works and cooperates with the bodywork. Lastly, chapter nine was defining the tool for Renewal Of The Mind and the various aspects and elements that would need to be addressed within compassionately healing the mind that would be later covered or reviewed on the worksheet (Appendix A) the tool for Renewal Of The Mind.

The tool addresses making sure that emotions are healed, thoughts are renewed, cycles are broken, true identity is understood, and then healthy coping mechanisms developed. These healthy coping mechanisms can be formed through bibliotherapy, gaining a renewed understanding of love, joy, humility, forgiveness, authenticity, prayer, obedience, and meekness. Prayerfully this tool (worksheet) and understanding will be used to empower counselors, believers, and individuals in understanding the Renewal Of The Mind that is required to dismantle addictions of all types.

In conclusion, this project has been several years of studying, and analyzing various resources to construct into an empowerment tool for the Body of Christ to assist with the epidemic of addictive behaviors that are no different from those found in the world. My prayer is that the combined exposure of the dichotomy of Renewal Of The Mind, its functions, and workings, along with these biblical aspects will be used to transform believers from worldly addictions to being completely addicted to the presence of God, the Lord Jesus Christ, and the Holy Spirit!

APPENDIX A: Worksheet for Renewal Of The Mind

APPENDIX A: RENEWAL OF THE MIND WORKSHEET

Believers individually, or with the assistance of a counselor, or in group therapy can work through the sections on this worksheet to be empowered with an understanding of the elements that need to be renewed in the mind to achieve freedom from addictions.
It is suggested to use a spiral notebook dedicated to journaling this journey of renewal.

As we embark upon this journey together, it is first imperative to recognize, empower, and draw from the Helper, The Holy Spirit, The Spirit of Truth to assist in the entire Renewal of the Mind process. You can do so by meditating on the following three scriptures regularly, and inviting Him into the healing and renewal process daily.
John 14:26, 16:8, 16:13 (all in the Amplified Classic Bible).

Realm of The Mind

- ☐ Meditate on the 2 theme scriptures for Renewal of the Mind and journal anything that stands out to you. Try reading them in several different versions of the bible.
- ☐ Romans 12:1-2
- ☐ 1 Thessalonians 5:23
- ☐ Identify the different functions of the mind/soul.
- ☐ Review the identified basic needs and note/highlight any areas that need special attention. See Gary Chapman's definition of the basic needs of mankind in Chapter One Early Formation.
- ☐ Review the list of scriptures to identify, and cleanse the conscience; recognizing the difference between the conscious and conscience. See Chapter One section on Conscience vs. Conscious text review.
- ☐ Define the role of guilt in the life of a believer, verses false guilt. Identify any areas of guilt that must be cleansed and healed.
- ☐ To expose any toxic memory structures in the subconscious mind, answer the following question: "What are the negative attributes of your childhood?"

- ☐ Meditate on 2 Corinthians 10:4-5 to expose strongholds (these are prejudices and preconceptions) that need to be pulled down and replaced with grace-filled thoughts as in Proverbs 1:8-9 TPT.

- ☐ Delve into and understand the role of feelings and emotions, to process them for what they are, yet not be led by them.

- ☐ Review the list of scriptures to identify the types of "mind" that are found in the Bible. See Chapter One section on Biblical Survey of Types of Mind.

Truth

- ☐ Invite the Holy Spirit to expose any lies and deception that you have believed, and have become a root cause for addictive behaviors.

Mind vs. Brain

- ☐ Understanding that the brain is the hardware of the soul, as well as the scientific functions of the brain can assist in dismantling addictions. Including the importance of communication and perception, which can be hindered by malfunctions of the brain and mind. See the Brain sections in Chapter Three and Chapter Seven.

Transformation

- ☐ Use the guidelines for transformation found in Chapter Four to assist in both behavioral change and cognitive behavior changes for renewal.

Possible Causes of Addiction

Check all areas that apply:

- ☐ Trauma - ACEs
- ☐ Damaged Emotions
- ☐ Depression
- ☐ Demonic Influence - Screwtape Element
- ☐ Denial
- ☐ Memory Repression
- ☐ People Pleasing
- ☐ Passiveness or Aggressiveness
- ☐ Orphan Spirit
- ☐ Conflict Avoidance
- ☐ Fragmented Soul
- ☐ Unresolved Anger

Types of Addictions

Check all areas that apply, be mindful to read the descriptions to discern all areas:

- ☐ **Substance Abuse**
  Description: Alcohol; Drugs (illegal and prescription)
- ☐ **Monetary Obsessions**
  Description: Excessive spending; Hoarding
- ☐ **Food Disorders**
  Description: Bulimia (binge-purge); Anorexia (self-starvation); Obesity caused by gluttony
- ☐ **Feeling Addictions**
  Description: Rage; Sadness; Fear; Excessive excitement; Religious righteousness; Joy fixation; People-pleasing, perfectionism; Legalism
- ☐ **Thought Addictions**
  Description: Excessive detailing; Worry; Nonstop talking; Lustful thoughts; Unsettled mind
- ☐ **Activity Obsessions**
  Description: Work; Sports; Reading; Gambling; Exercise; Television viewing; Owning and caring for excessive numbers of pets
- ☐ **Will Addictions**
  Description: Controlling; Controlled; Reenactment addicts; Caretaker

The Brain And Addictions

- ☐ Understand that the brain can be re-wired, re-programmed, renewed through epigentics.
- ☐ Gain an understanding of how dopamine impacts decisions and behavior.

Bodywork

- Regularly pray over the systems of the body. See Chapter Eight section on Healing Systems regarding engaging in meditative prayer over the various systems for healing.

- Gain a further understanding of the role of dopamine and natural ways to balance dopamine levels. See Chapter Eight section on Another Look At Dopamine.

Areas of Renewal

- Healed Emotions
- Renewed Thoughts
- Breaking Cycles
- Identity

Healthy Coping Mechanisms

- Bibliotherapy
- Prayer
- Obedience And Meekness
- Love
- Forgiveness
- Humility
- Joy
- Authenticity

Combined Bibliography

"Articles - Health Information | Cleveland Clinic." Cleveland Clinic. Accessed March 16, 2023. https://my.clevelandclinic.org/health/articles.

"Dictionary by Merriam-Webster: America's Most-trusted Online Dictionary." Dictionary by Merriam-Webster: America's Most-trusted Online Dictionary. Accessed June 1, 2021. https://www.merriam-webster.com/dictionary.

"Dopamine: What It Is, Function & Symptoms." Cleveland Clinic. Last modified March 23, 2023. https://my.clevelandclinic.org/health/articles/22581-dopamine.

"Drugs, Brains, and Behavior: The Science of Addiction." National Institute on Drug Abuse. Last modified May 30, 2023. https://nida.nih.gov/research-topics/addiction-science/drugs-brain-behavior-science-of-addiction.

"NIMH Mental Illness." NIMH Home. Accessed April 26, 2021. https://www.nimh.nih.gov/health/statistics/mental-illness.shtml.

Alger, Wanda. Oracles of Grace: Building a Legacy of Wisdom and Revelation. Alger Publications, 2017.

Allen, James. As a Man Thinketh. Amazon, 2014. Kindle Edition.

Amen, Daniel G. Change Your Brain, Change Your Life: The Breakthrough Program for Conquering Anxiety, Depression, Obsessiveness, Anger, and Impulsiveness. New York: Harmony, 2015. Revised and Expanded

Amen, Daniel. Healing the Hardware of the Soul: Enhance Your Brain to Improve Your Work, Love, and Spiritual Life. New York: Simon & Schuster, 2008.

Amen, Tana. The Relentless Courage of a Scared Child: How Persistence, Grit, and Faith Created a Reluctant Healer. Nashville: Thomas Nelson, 2021.

Anderson, Neil T. Winning the Battle Within: Realistic Steps to Overcoming Sexual Strongholds. Eugene, OR: Harvest House Pub, 2008.

Arterburn, Stephen, and David A. Stoop. When Someone You Love is Someone You Hate. W Publishing Group, 1988.

Beall, James L., and Marjorie Barber. Laying the Foundation. Bridge Logos Fndtn, 1976.

Beaty, Cooper. "Lesson 11." Lecture, Principles of Learning And Teaching Methods, Rhema Bible Training College, Broken Arrow, OK, October 22, 2003.

Beaty, Cooper. "Lesson 4." Lecture, Principles of Learning And Teaching Methods, Rhema Bible Training College, Broken Arrow, OK, September 19, 2003.

Beaty, Cooper. "Lesson 5." Lecture, Principles of Learning And Teaching Methods, Rhema Bible Training College, Broken Arrow, OK, September 29, 2003.

Beaty, Cooper. "Lesson 7." Lecture, Principles of Learning And Teaching Methods, Rhema Bible Training College, Broken Arrow, OK, October 8, 2003.

Bible Search and Study Tools - Blue Letter Bible. Accessed April 4, 2021. https://www.blueletterbible.org/.

Bible Search and Study Tools - Blue Letter Bible. Accessed July 26, 2023. https://www.blueletterbible.org/.

Braden, Gregg. The Divine Matrix: Bridging Time, Space, Miracles, and Belief. Carlsbad: Hay House, 2007.

Chapman, Gary D. Desperate Marriages: Moving Toward Hope and Healing in Your Relationship. Chicago: Northfield Pub, 2008.

Clinton, Tim, Archibald D. Hart, and George Ohlschlager. Caring for People God's Way: Personal and Emotional Issues, Addictions, Grief, and Trauma. Nelson Reference & Electronic Publishing, 2005.

Collins, Gary R. Christian Counseling: A Comprehensive Guide. W Publishing Group, 1988. Combined Edition

Crabb, Larry. Fully Alive: A Biblical Vision of Gender That Frees Men and Women to Live Beyond Stereotypes. Grand Rapids: Baker Books, 2013. Kindle edition

Denise, Paulette. Christians On Assignment Talking About Obedience. Houston: A Portion, 2010.

Denise, Paulette. Renewal of the Mind! According to Romans 12:2. A Portion Ministries, 2014.

Digest, Reader's, Reader's Digest Editors, and Of Readers Digest Editors. ABC's of the Human Mind: A Family Answer Book. New York: Readers Digest, 1990.

Dillon, Brandy, and Dionne Davis. Come Forth: Transformational Principles to Arise from Life's Afflictions. Raleigh: PENDIUM, 2018.

Frangipane, Francis. The Three Battlegrounds: An In-Depth View of the Three Arenas of Spiritual Warfare: the Mind, the Church and the Heavenly Places, 2nd ed. Cedar Rapids: Arrow Publications, 2010.

Fredrickson, Renee. Repressed Memories: A Journey to Recovery from Sexual Abuse. New York: Simon & Schuster, 1992.

Gallagher, Steve. A Biblical Guide to Counseling the Sexual Addict. Dry Ridge: Steve Gallagher, 2005.

Garland, Desiree. *Encode: Praying with the Language of Glory*, 1st ed. Amazon Kindle Direct Publishing, 2020. Kindle edition.

Gray, John. *Win from Within: Finding Yourself by Facing Yourself*. FaithWords, 2018.

Grenz, Stanley J. *Theology for the Community of God*. Grand Rapids: Wm. B. Eerdmans Publishing, 2000.

Hart, Archibald D. *Unlocking the Mystery of Your Emotions*. W Publishing Group, 1989.

Hawkins, David R. *Power vs. Force: The Hidden Determinants of Human Behavior*. Carlsbad: Hay House, 2013. Kindle Edition.

Heiser, Michael S. *The Unseen Realm: Recovering the Supernatural Worldview of the Bible*. Lexham Press, 2015.

Hopkins, Ivory. *Who Counsels The Counselor: Building and Restoring Leaders*. Scotts Valley: Createspace Independent Publishing Platform, 2019.

Hunt, June. *Codependency: Balancing an Unbalanced Relationship*. Rose Publishing, 2013.

Hunt, June. *Critical Spirit: Confronting the Heart of a Critic*, 7th ed. Peabody, MA: Hendrickson Publishers, 2017.

Hunt, June. *Guilt: Living Guilt-Free*. Peabody: Aspire Press, 2013.

Hunt, June. *How to Defeat Harmful Habits: Freedom from Six Addictive Behaviors*. Harvest House Pub, 2011.

Idleman, Shane. *Help! I'm Addicted: Overcoming the Cravings that Overcome You*. El Paseo Publications, 2019. Kindle Edition.

Jantz, Gregory. *Social Media and Depression: How to Be Healthy and Happy in the Digital Age*. Peabody: Aspire Press, 2021.

Karr-Morse, Robin, and Meredith S. Wiley. *Scared Sick: The Role of Childhood Trauma in Adult Disease*. New York, Basic Books, 2012.

Koch, Ruth N., and Kenneth C. Haugk. *Speaking the Truth in Love: How to be an Assertive Christian*. St Louis: Stephen Ministries St Louis, 1992.

LaHaye, Tim. *Spirit-controlled Temperament*. Carol Stream: Tyndale House Publishers, 1993.

Leaf, Caroline. *Cleaning Up Your Mental Mess: 5 Simple, Scientifically Proven Steps to Reduce Anxiety, Stress, and Toxic Thinking*. Ada: Baker Books, 2021.

Leaf, Caroline. *Switch On Your Brain: The Key to Peak Happiness, Thinking, and Health*. Ada: Baker Books, 2013.

Leaf, Caroline. The Perfect You: A Blueprint for Identity. Ada: Baker Books, 2017.

Lewis, Clive S. The Screwtape Letters; With, Screwtape Proposes a Toast. Scribner Paper Fiction, 1982.

MacArthur, John F. Worship: The Ultimate Priority. Chicago: Moody Publishers, 2012.

Mental Healthcare Clinic Focusing On Your Brain Health | Dr. Amen. Accessed March 3, 2023. https://www.amenclinics.com/.

Meyer, Joyce. Beauty for Ashes: Receiving Emotional Healing. Fenton: FaithWords, 2003.

Nee, Watchman. The Spiritual Man. New York: Christian Fellowship Publishers Inc, 1977.

Nelson, Bradley, and Ric Thompson. The Heart of the Emotion Code: Dr. Bradley Nelson on the Effects of Emotional Energy on our Health and Success. Healthy Wealthy nWise Press, 2014. Kindle Edition.

Null, William G. Rejection - Its Fruits and Its Roots: A Scriptural Understanding of Rejection, How it Works and How to Minister. Kirkwood, MO: Impact Christian Books Inc, 2005.

Pittman, Catherine M., and Elizabeth M. Karle. Rewire Your Anxious Brain: How to Use the Neuroscience of Fear to End Anxiety, Panic and Worry. Oakland: New Harbinger Publications Inc, 2015.

Prince, Derek. Pulling Down Strongholds. Charlotte: Whitaker House, 2013.

Prince, Derek. Spiritual Warfare. Charlotte: Whitaker House, 2001.

Rogers, Gayle. Healing The Traumatized Soul. AuthorHouse, 2005.

Rogers, Gayle. The Whole Soul: Rescripting Your Life for Personal Transformation. Kingdom House Publishing, 2014.

Rohr, Richard, and Mike Morrell. The Divine Dance: The Trinity and Your Transformation. Whitaker House, 2016. Kindle edition.

Sandford, John L., and Paula Sandford. Healing the Wounded Spirit. Victory House Publishers, 1985.

Sanford, John A. The Kingdom Within: The Inner Meaning of Jesus' Sayings. HarperOne, 1987.

Seamands, David A. Healing for Damaged Emotions. Wheaton: David C Cook, 1991.

Skurja, Catherine. Paradox Lost: Uncovering the True Identity in Christ. Imago Dei Resources LLC, 2012.

Stearns, Robert. The Cry of Mordecai: Awakening an Esther Generation in a Haman Age. Shippensburg: Destiny Image Pub, 2009.

Sudduth, William. Deliverance Training Manual. RAM Inc., 2013.

Thieme , R. B., Jr. Satan and Demonism, 3rd ed. Houston, TX: R. B. Thieme, Jr., Bible Ministries, 1996.

Tolman, Kay. Moved with Compassion: A New Wineskin for Healing and Deliverance. 2017.

Trayser, John R. The Aces Revolution!: The Impact of Adverse Childhood Experiences. Scotts Valley: Createspace Independent Publishing Platform, 2016.

Trulin, Paul G. Dr. Paul G. Trulin's My Body, His Life, 11th ed. Sacramento: Paul Trulin Ministries, 1989.

Turabian, Kate L. A Manual for Writers of Research Papers, Theses, and Dissertations: Chicago Style for Students and Researchers, 9th ed. Chicago: University of Chicago Press, 2018.

Turner, Paulette D. "Identity Conference via Zoom." Conference session presented at Double Portion Kingdom Ministries, Houston, TX, April 7, 2021.

Youssef, Nada. "The Realities of Addiction with Psychiatrist Dr. David Streem." Cleveland Clinic. Last modified December 5, 2018. https://my.clevelandclinic.org/podcasts/health-essentials/the-realities-of-addiction-with-psychiatrist-dr-david-streem.

www.ingramcontent.com/pod-product-compliance
Lightning Source LLC
Chambersburg PA
CBHW081354290426
44110CB00018B/2376